SAFARI PRESS

Season of Obsession

Season of Obsession

by

Joel Spring

SAFARI PRESS INC.

The trademark Safari Press ® is registered with the U.S. Patent and Trademark Office and in other countries.

Spring, Joel

First edition

Safari Press Inc.

2000, Long Beach, California

ISBN 1-57157-170-1

Library of Congress Catalog Card Number: 99-66842

10 9 8 7 6 5 4 3 2 1

Readers wishing to receive the Safari Press catalog, featuring many fine books on big-game hunting, wingshooting, and sporting firearms, should write to Safari Press Inc., P.O. Box 3095, Long Beach, CA 90803, USA. Tel: (714) 894-9080 or visit our Web site at www.safaripress.com.

TABLE OF CONTENTS

DEDICATION

This is for Greta.

ACKNOWLEDGMENTS

For their invaluable assistance in the process of editing this book, many thanks to Wendy Wehner and Vicki Vest.

For a decade of support, I would like to thank Pat Durkin and the rest of the staff, past and present, at Deer & Deer Hunting *magazine.*

For their patience and thoughtfulness, thanks to Ludo Wurfbain, Stacy Davies, and B. J. Lambert at Safari Press.

For the gift of reading and a lifetime of encouragement, I owe a great debt to my parents, Marvin and Jayne Spring.

INTRODUCTION

"You are obsessed." I get that a lot. From friends. From family. From coworkers. Just yesterday, I found out pheasant season had been switched from the third week in October to the first. My vacation had been scheduled for the third week so I could bird hunt. What to do? Rather than change the vacation, I decided to keep it where it was, realizing I already had a long weekend for the new pheasant opener. By the third week—my vacation—I'll be worn out from bird hunting, having devoted every free minute after work that I can to it, and ready for a few leisurely days of deer hunting with the bow in the Catskills. Of course, that means I'll have to start making travel plans and figuring out who can go and when and how and what the moon will be like, and how the apples and the acorns are this year and so on and so on. As I was puzzling over schedules and calendars yesterday, making calls and sending e-mails, my boss walked into the office, shaking his head sadly and repeating the familiar phrase. "Do you know you're worrying about something that isn't even going to happen for another four months? You are obsessed," he said, with no small amount of pity.

OK, I am. And it never really ends. Even after the last shot has been shot, and the last gun has been cleaned and put away, and the last of the venison has been eaten, the obsession continues. There are always more plans to be made, more dreams to be dreamed. It's a full-time job—as if I needed another one. Did I mention the caribou hunt I am planning exactly 485 days from now? You can't start obsessing too soon, you know.

Prelude

Something in the wind speaks to me.
Something in me hears.

August 10—The Dogs

I feel bad for the dogs, especially Maggie. I wonder if Maggie understands. I know the season is coming. I can feel the slightly cooler nights and shorter days and I'm sure the dogs can, too. But unlike them, I have a calendar at eye level. I know the time of the year I live the rest of the year waiting for—hunting season. It is only a few days away. Maggie, on the other hand, must really wonder what happened. One day last winter we were happily chasing rabbits and grouse and the next, the guns were cleaned and put away. The tired old clothes were relegated to the back of the basement closet. The whistles and leashes were tucked into the back of my hunting vest, now hanging forgotten in the back hallway. The piles of shells in my truck that gave it a rather volatile quality were placed back in boxes—some even in the *right* boxes— in yet another corner of the basement. That was months ago. The last day of the last season—rabbit season—was five months ago, an eternity in a dog's life, I should think. I wonder if she thinks hunting season has ended forever.

Sometimes, especially in August, I feel that way.

Ted doesn't know. The Lab is still a pup and hasn't spent even a single season chasing pheasants and ducks, rabbits and squirrels, grouse and woodcock. He'll learn these things this year or start learning, anyway. For now, Ted thinks hunting is chasing a training dummy across the backyard. Every now and then I'll load a shotgun with blanks and take him for practice by the lake, if I can find the time. These are just puppy adventures, though. Ted doesn't know any differently. He doesn't yet know about the hunt. He doesn't know about its insanity and elation and exhaustion. He doesn't know about the obsession.

Mag knows, though. She knows of cackling roosters and flushing woodcock. Of mind-bending chases along thorny and hidden corridors. She knows the things I know, and much more. She knows what happens down on the ground when a big rooster runs along under the cover of the saw grass. She sees what happens when crisscrossing air currents betray a fat woodcock. She knows a shot—not necessarily a good shot—is likely to follow. She knows where a field mouse has passed and where deer have bedded down for the night. She smells in color and hears in frequencies of which I can only dream. She is my nose, my ears, my eyes, and a big piece of my heart. I've seen her dreaming of the hunt and I wonder if her dreams are as vivid as mine. I've watched her twitching legs and flexing muscles and endless sniffing, suspecting *her* dreams may be even better. I wonder if she smells the rich scent of the wild birds in her dreams. I imagine she does.

Every time a shotgun comes out of the safe, she hops up on the couch next to me to inspect it, looking from it to me, waiting for a sign that this might be the day when the dreadful wait is over. She cocks her head and listens intently each time the word "bird" comes up in a phone conversation. She watches me closely to make sure I don't put on the "real" hunting clothes without her noticing. Not the Training Clothes, but the Hunting Clothes. She knows the difference and, like me, she waits. I know it's only sixteen more days, but as far as Maggie is concerned it may be a lifetime away. Or maybe she does know it's right around the corner.

Maybe she can smell it.

August 21—Confirmation

A week later in the Adirondacks with Howard, my father-in-law, I'm on my favorite kind of fishing trip—the kind that's thrown together at the last minute. A phone call, a quick packing job and a hasty lashing of the canoe to the truck, a poorly planned stop by the supermarket for necessities like sardines, hotdogs, and beer, and we are on the way. After a few rainy hours on the road, we are in the wilderness. With no campsites available at the state parks, we situate our tent in the woods on a bank high above West Canada Creek.

The small opening in the tall yellow birches overlooks a sportsman's dream. Surveying the wide creek below and the twin round mountains in the distance (Howard has a good name for them), we decide that a finer view could not be bought for ten bucks a night at some overcrowded state-run campsite. We swear if the bears don't get us tonight, we'll come back to this very same spot next spring.

Spending the entire day casting worms at the native brookies, we take a good many from the opaque, tea-colored pools—backwaters that may be a foot deep, or perhaps sixty. Our only indication of what's going on below the surface of the creek is when the gaudy orange and red bobbers gently dance on the quiet water, signaling the presence of yet another brook trout. The memories of days I've spent in the lower reaches of this creek in the spring, casting fancy flies to finicky brown trout, have nothing over the simple bobber rigs and globs of worms and the gloriously colorful wild brookies. Stealth and snobbery need not apply here. Simplicity already has the job.

This first night in the mountains—not too far from home, but a world away—we roast some brookies over the fire and toast the creek with a beer. Later on, after dousing the lantern and smothering the campfire, we gaze up into the night sky. The moon is nearly full, yet the depth of the stars is dizzying. For a moment, with my head thrown back in the lawn chair, I swear I'm looking down instead of up. Sitting like that for a few hours, we talk about everything and nothing. We point out satellites to each other and wonder what this or that star is. The conversation waxes and wanes. Thoughts, clean and simple, fill in the large areas the words leave empty.

After a particularly long stretch of silence, Howard turns to me, saying simply, "It's right around the corner, you know."

To an outsider the statement might seem detached, senseless, its meaning as oblique as the murky bottom of the West Canada. I know what he's talking about, though, realizing what he's been thinking in the silent moments. They're the same things I've been thinking about. I'm looking forward to the first of September and goose season and the odd squirrel hunt, now only a week away. Howard, however, who hunts only deer, is seeing all the way into November. His time. Still three months away, yes, but for impractical people like him and me, right around the corner. It's not far away at all.

I nod, looking back up to the sky. Howard's simple statement hangs in the cooling air, requiring no follow-up. He knows I know what he meant. Closing my eyes, I feel the cool breeze, carried across the big creek from the north, and sense a hint of autumn in its breath. A pair of coyotes wail from the twin hills that are now barely visible against the moonlit sky. It's a long time before I sleep, and when I do, I dream many dreams. Though I won't remember what they were about, I know the dreams are not of August.

September 1—Prelude

It's dawn of the first day of hunting season. My wife, Greta, and I are deep in squirrel territory—or at least as deep as you can get in a forty-acre wood lot. Cornfields, yet uncut, reach to the woods on the west and south sides. The timber, loaded with oak and beech and peppered with hickory and walnut, has always provided a bounty of fat bushytails.

Earlier, just at daylight, we walked along the edge of the vast cornfield, suddenly hearing a loud rustling in the stalks to our left. We froze, wondering if a pheasant or an unsuspecting squirrel was making the commotion. I started to say something to Greta and she shushed me just as a big white-tailed doe quietly emerged from the corn. Only thirty yards away, the doe moved casually across the opening before spotting us and stopping. It stood there for a moment, curious, but not scared enough to stop chewing its mouthful of corn. Giving us a quick head bob, it calmly crossed to the thorn apple thicket on our right. Greta and I passed a silent look that simply said, "Nice way to start the morning."

But now, with my back against a big beech, it's all I can do to sit still. I glance over at Greta, who's still patiently watching the treetops. I close my eyes to block out the bugs and doze off for a few minutes, lulled to sleep by the low thrumming of farm machinery off in the distance. When I awake, there's a chickadee on the branch in front of me, not two feet from my face. It cocks its head at me like a dog before flying off into the warm morning. Scratching the back of my neck, I feel a new crop of welts there. Maybe the chickadee was coming to feast on the bugs that were feasting on me.

After an hour or so, the humidity in the woods becomes unbearable. We get up just to feel the breeze across our faces as we slowly move through the woods. After walking half the length of the wood lot, we're greeted by a familiar sound. Somewhere above us in a giant beech a squirrel is cutting nuts, shaking the leaf-covered limbs sixty feet up. We hear the *chomp chomp* as its teeth cut through the sinewy stems holding the nuts. Hearing beechnuts hitting the ground, we approach the great tree. The squirrel grows silent. Sitting down, we wait for twenty minutes, but it never comes down. Greta walks off through the woods as I sit down by the beech tree, hoping the squirrel might see her going and come back out for me.

A moment later I nearly jump out of my skin when the twenty-two cracks twice behind me. Quickly walking into the beech saplings, I search for my wife. She's standing under a twenty-foot beech, searching the ground.

"So?" I ask.

"So, is this rifle sighted in or not?" she asks, holding the old Marlin out to me.

"Um, I never shot it. It's one my dad passed along to us last year."

"It's off," she declares flatly, still searching the ground for a squirrel that we never find.

I offer her my .410.

"No thanks, maybe it's just me." I can tell by her voice she doesn't really think so. I wish she'd take the shotgun, but I think she'd like to remind me what a good shot she is. I wisely stifle a giggle as we head back into the more open woods. If she catches me laughing, only one of us might come out of the woods at noon.

Around noon, we're in the corner of the woods we haven't touched yet. It's one little finger of oaks sticking into the cornfield and it's always been a good spot on a slow day. Sitting for only a moment, I spot a squirrel running in the small trees on the edge of the corn. I point it out to Greta, who has her back to it. When it becomes clear the squirrel doesn't intend to come any closer, we move in, stepping gingerly but quickly in the moldy carpet of leaves. Greta takes the lead.

Standing where we last saw the squirrel, we wait no longer than a minute before we surprise it coming out of the corn. Spotting us at the same time, it races to the top of the only decent-sized oak around. It pauses high up on the tree trunk to check us out and I hear the safety of the Marlin slide off. I watch the motionless squirrel while my wife takes aim.

Once again she misses and the squirrel zips to the other side of the tree. "Here," she says, handing me the rifle with one hand and abruptly relieving me of my shotgun with the other. This time I can't stifle a snicker. "I'll go around."

It takes a long minute to break through the old vines that have choked the saplings on the edge of the field. Finally stumbling into the corn, I immediately spot the squirrel. It's now ten feet higher in the young oak. I whistle and wave my arms, trying to scare it back to Greta's side so she can shoot. It won't budge.

After a moment, Greta yells, "If you have a shot, shoot!"

I take careful aim with the old relic, placing the buckhorn sights squarely across the back of the squirrel's head. I steadily squeeze the trigger, watching a piece of bark fly off the tree at the sound of the shot. The squirrel scampers back to the other side, untouched. The .410 roars and the previously lucky squirrel tumbles to earth.

Back inside the woods my wife is holding the squirrel at arm's length by its toe, waiting for me to put it in my game bag. She smiles and says, "Now let's get out of here—it's too hot for this. And by the way," she adds, "I told you that gun was off."

By evening, a rainstorm has come and gone, draining the sky of some of its humidity. With the kids still happy at Grandma's house, we hike to the ponds, looking for geese. Although goose season started today, this is really just a scouting mission. I have traded the lithe .410 for my heavy old Winchester 12-gauge pump and a box of steel number ones. The first pond—a brush-choked mess—is our secret hole for wood ducks. With a few hours of daylight remaining, we decide to check it out. The cooler air has slowed the mosquitoes down, but the wall of brush between us and the pond proves nearly impenetrable. Finally reaching the pond, we've made so much noise breaking branches it's no surprise when there aren't any ducks sitting on it. We hastily head toward the other pond out in the middle of the open field.

My heart sinks as we cross the old railroad bed and start into the field. The other pond is a tragedy, a casualty of the visionless farmer who owns it. The thin rows of trees once lining the edge have been pushed in with an excavator. All that remains are piles of discarded hardwood. It's not even cut for firewood. I wonder if the pound-foolish farmer has any idea how many thousands of dollars in hardwood are lying there rotting so he can have a few more bushels of corn next year.

Damn.

The trees used to form a nearly full circle around the pond. The small area that had no trees was a funnel through which the geese and ducks would take off and land. Now, with all of the edge cover lost, I can't imagine a duck or goose ever wanting to land here again. Somehow even the water, once teeming with bass and bluegills, looks ruined. A sickly bluish-gray, it smells like death. At the far side, the old spillway has been bulldozed in, and the ditch that used to feed the pond has been diverted. The pond has effectively been choked of its life. To think someone actually planned this makes me want to retch. Thinking of the flocks of geese and ducks that used to sit here, and the herons that fished the banks, I can almost see the dimples on the surface the bass and bluegills would make on nights like this.

Tonight, the surface is untouched by life.

I saw the machinery out here this summer but had no idea the carnage was on such a grand scale. This is where the tree huggers and so-called conservationists should be staging their demonstrations, but no one is going to report this. Nothing dramatic here. Just an entire ecosystem ruined. Gone. Destroyed.

Not front page news by any means. No one will be up in arms. No attention whatsoever will be paid. Nobody to mourn for the dead pond. It's nothing but a cesspool now.

Greta and I search for a secluded spot to sit among the upturned root piles and butchered trunks. Last week, I noticed one of the nearby cornfields was cut. I was hoping the geese would be flying back and forth between the pond and the cut field. Even if they ignore the pond, maybe the geese will still come to the field. My hope springs eternal.

We flush a fat young rooster pheasant on the bank of the murky pond as we step around the emaciated carcass of a snapping turtle. Shouldering the Winchester, I lead the bird, taking an imaginary shot. But my heart's not in it.

Sitting on the edge of the pond, we face west into the sunset. The sky's colors are dazzling. I love the mountains, but there is nothing like a flatland sunset. The beauty of the sky and the quiet conversation with my wife bring the first evening of the season to a tranquil close. In the last moments of blood-red daylight, a dozen wood ducks fly over, passing thirty or forty yards from our hideout. Briefly setting their wings over the stained water, they think better of it. Picking up speed, they fly to the other pond—the brush-choked one.

There is a sadness in the beating of their wings.

The Early Season

*The warmth holds on
as Summer strains to keep her grip.
She won't last long
against the cold insistence.
She will Fall.*

September 7—The Goose Field

Shining the flashlight around the cornfield, I decide our little flock looks good. The highlights of white tail feathers on the big decoys shine in the dark field. The spread looks so good I have already had to put Ted on the leash. After about twenty shells were set, we discovered that he was following along behind me and attacking them, knocking them off their metal stakes. By the end of the week, even the sight of the plastic birds will make him go crazy with anticipation, but today these giant "field birds" are all new to him. Although we had no need for a retriever in this tiny patch of cut corn, I couldn't see leaving Ted home. If nothing else, he's good company.

Arriving far too early, we set the spread of decoys out, then put an old blanket in the middle of them to lie on. Unfurling the camo net that will go over us, we unleash Ted. The trouble is, it's still an hour until dawn. After ten or fifteen minutes, John is fast asleep and Ted does a good job of imitating John's snoring.

Daylight is merely a splotch of murky dawn on the dark horizon when I stand to look over the decoys again. Suddenly, Ted is racing past me. My goofy and eternally happy black Lab has his hackles up and is growling in a ferocious baritone I've never heard before. Grabbing blindly, I somehow snag his collar

Few things are more exciting than seeing geese coming toward the decoys.

on the way by and am thrown to my knees. It's like grabbing the door handle of a moving freight car.

"Whoa, Ted, *whoa!*"

I manage to right myself, still holding the dog. I have him by the collar, but he is up on his hind legs growling and aggressively straining against my hold. The back of his head is nearly at eye level. Suddenly, I realize how big my little black puppy has gotten.

"What's wrong?" John asks, coming up behind me.

"I dunno. Maybe a coon. Or a deer."

Peering down past the edge of the cornfield, we strain to see into the tangle of briars where Ted's attention is focused. He's no longer growling loudly, but I can still feel the vibrations from his vocal cords through the collar. Reaching for the leash, I snap it on him again. Suddenly, a pinpoint of light winks on and we're shocked it's only thirty yards from us. Two figures approach in the dark.

"Are you guys gonna hunt here?" a voice from behind the light asks.

Later on, John and I will joke about what we should have said. "No, we set all these goose decoys out because we like them, and we're here so early because they are most beautiful when viewed by dawn's early light, while lying in a muddy field."

"Yeah, are you?" John asks, still sounding sleepy.

"Well, we don't have decoys, but we're just going to sit in the brush on the side of the field. Do you mind?"

"No, just don't shoot us," John jokes.

"OK," the dark figure says dully, "no problem."

There must be *some* problem because the two of them hesitate by the edge, raising their voices at each other. Walking out to the road, they climb into a van and leave. The whole thing seems odd. Oh, well. At least I can let Ted loose.

"I guess you weren't the only one watching the field, John."

"Nope, guess not. Those birds are here every day and someone else was bound to notice."

As first light drifts onto the field, I realize just how close we are to civilization. I clearly see the main road, a hundred yards from us. The field lies nestled between two houses. They're not extremely close but not all *that* far away. We came in from the woods below in the dark, and, now that it is light enough to see, the proximity to the road is what startles me. I begin questioning the somewhat suburban setting when John quiets me.

"There's geese here. What more do you want?"

As we load the shotguns, the sun peeks out behind us, just touching the far edge of the corn stubble. Cars begin passing on the road. People are on their way to work. Sitting out in the middle of the field, I feel absolutely ridiculous. With two grown men and a dog sitting on a blanket, we look like some kind of warped picnic. At least we're dressed in camo and should be inconspicuous to the passing cars.

Wrong. At a quarter-past seven, a blue van slows on the road and the driver's side window slides down. It's John's best friend, Paul, who owns one of the houses next to the field. No. Oh, please. *Not this.*

"Hey look at the fairies on the blanket," he yells at the top of his lungs. "Aren't you two just so CUTE!" The van roars off.

"This is beautiful, John, just perfect."

"Any minute now," he says, searching the sky, ignoring me and smiling.

Fifteen minutes later, I'm standing up to stretch when John says *"Geese! Get down now!"* Diving for the blanket, I glimpse a dozen or more birds over the woods at the west end of the field. Ted, who's been peacefully curled up on the blanket, hears their honking, quickly sitting upright. Only a hundred yards from us, the geese already have their wings set. Pulling the camo mesh over ourselves and Ted, we lie flat on our backs. But Ted wants nothing to do with it. As the geese close the distance, he struggles to sit up under the netting, a big black flounder caught in a net. I throw a leg over his back as John wraps an arm around his neck. Our guns lie useless at our sides on the blanket.

The geese are getting close—*extremely* close—and I want to grab my Winchester. "Wait, wait . . . wait," John is chanting insanely at my side.

I'm in awe at the size of the geese coasting toward us. My heart is pounding a strange staccato beat. This is nothing *at all* like duck hunting. I feel like a docked ship at Pearl Harbor with the Zeroes closing fast. They seem about to hit us when John finally says, "*Now!*"

We sit up to begin shooting, but of course it's not that simple. The front bead on John's shotgun hangs up in the camo, and as I take aim at the lead bird, my partner is wrestling with the netting. Ted is out like a shot. Miraculously, John frees himself in time to join me in shooting at the birds, now flaring away but only twenty yards from us. Selecting one of the nearest birds, I lead, shoot, shoot, and shoot again as John does the same. The big birds, now gaining speed, climb and pass over the road, a few feathers drifting down behind them.

"What the hell?" I ask. "I *had* that bird!"

"Damned steel shot," John says. Reloading, he quickly adds, "Here they come again!"

Quickly jamming three shells into the gun, I lie back down. The geese are coming back. Thirty yards from us, Ted stands in the open field looking up at them. It's too late to grab him. Passing the end of the field sixty yards from us, one of the geese, a big gander, simply wobbles and falls out of the flock, crashing into the field! Ted races for the lifeless goose with John in hot pursuit. The immobile pile of feathers suddenly rises, throwing its neck in Ted's direction. He stops six feet away from the huge bird, hitting the brakes so hard he nearly somersaults. The goose's neck weaves around like an angry cobra, and the young dog, having absolutely no idea what he's doing, darts in and grabs the bird by the wing. In a bizarre scene my Lab begins dragging the big gander, who's still on his feet, slowly back toward John. By now I'm on my feet racing for Ted, fearing the goose is going to tear him up. Fortunately for both bird and dog, it soon falls over dead. Ted continues dragging the gander down the field toward John, who relieves him of the chore. When Ted runs to my side, I praise him highly for his first successful—if somewhat unconventional—retrieve.

An hour later, it's pouring rain as we sip coffee out of John's old green Thermos, watching the sky. A flock of geese that passed us twice on the far horizon suddenly turns our way. As we reach for the camo, a New York State Trooper car parks by the field.

"Oh no," I say, watching the geese approaching from the north, the trooper from the west.

"Joel, we're legal and we didn't do anything wrong. Don't worry," John says. His face says something different.

I suggest it might be wise to go meet the trooper halfway instead of making him walk across the muddy field in the rain. Unloading our guns and leashing Ted, we rise from the mud and meet the trooper. We watch helplessly as the geese pass over the far end of the field and, seeing all the commotion, move off.

"Morning, fellas," the trooper says, rain pouring off his plastic-covered Stetson.

"Morning, Officer, is there a problem?" John asks, cutting to the chase.

"I don't think so," he says, not smiling. "The people across the road heard shooting and called us. They're not complaining, just asking what anyone would be shooting this time of year. May I assume," he gestures dramatically at the decoys, "that you'd be hunting geese?"

Checking our licenses and engaging in a little chat, he asks to see the bird. As we walk him down the field and through the woods to where the truck is parked, it quickly becomes apparent that his reasons for wanting to see the goose are not official ones. As we walk, he just wants to talk hunting. At the back of my truck, he gazes at the huge bird that seems to take up the whole backseat. He picks the goose's fist-sized head up and turns it from side to side. His regulation demeanor fades. Suddenly, he's just one of the guys.

"Yeah . . ." he says, looking off, "I used to hunt a lot. Used to have the time, you know." For a moment, he is gone, completely lost in thought. There is a long silence. "Thanks, gentlemen, and good luck." He disappears back into the woods.

"Let's go," John says. "Won't be any birds back here for a few days."

"I've got time. . . ."

"I'm telling you, that's it for today," he insists.

Since John's been right at least twice this morning, I agree. It's already mid-morning. Gathering up the flock and the "blanket blind" we make the short drive to John's house for some badly needed coffee. Once out of the truck, we are treated to the sound of honking geese. A flock of geese—a huge flock—soars over John's driveway, heading for the field we just left. Without a word we jump into my truck. Passing the field on the road, we view the unearthly sight of over a hundred Canadas sitting among the very cornstalks where we had hidden. Had we stayed, they would have landed all around us. We missed them by no more than ten minutes. The smart thing to do would be to let them feed peacefully on the stubble today and then return tomorrow to try to kill a few.

What we do, of course, is not the smart thing.

As we wheel down through Paul's backyard and into the woods, the questionable suspension in my truck is bounced to its limit. Getting out—actually, falling out—I hastily tie Ted to the bumper. We race through a little abandoned orchard and up to the edge of the field. Hidden by a band of sumacs, we watch the geese feeding quietly seventy yards out. Behind us, Ted's pathetic, whimpering cries waft through the woods.

"What do you want to do?" John asks.

"Well, we could try rushing the field . . ." I suggest, mulling over the short list of other options.

The mulling lasts only a moment. A plan (not a good plan, but a plan) quickly forms. John crawls down through the sumac, and I wait for his signal. Raising his hand, he starts the race. A branch whacks me in the head and rips my cap off as I charge into the field.

I bog down in the mud. John, a little more fleet of foot, has a thirty-yard advantage, but the great flock lifts to the sky untouched, quickly disappearing over the woods. Still holding his gun out in front of him like a minuteman, John is laughing.

"What the hell are we doing?" he says bending over, out of breath.

"I thought you knew."

"Wrong again!"

From behind us, I'm again aware of Ted's pitiful barking. He's got to be wondering if John and I have lost our minds.

He's not the only one.

September 10—The Game Comes Home

We hoped the mama bunny would come back. We really did. Kneeling in the wet grass by the kids' swing set, Greta and I know she's not going to. At this point, letting nature take its course is out of the question. Besides, nature had very little to do with Ted's digging the nest up the other night. It wasn't nature's fault I should have been home weed-whacking around the swing set this summer instead of trout fishing. After three nights without the mother's return, the little gerbil-sized bunnies are skin and bone. It's rescue them now or face the ugly consequences of explaining what happened to them to my two young daughters.

With Greta holding the flashlight, I scoop the sorry little cottontails up and place them in my bait bucket, now comfortably lined with a bath towel. She and I exchange a mutual sigh. *Been here, done this.*

The first two nights (with rabbit season only a few weeks away) we feed the bunnies every few hours. It's like having babies all over again. We squirt a soupy mixture of Karo syrup and milk into each of their little rabbit mouths until it flows out the sides. At first, as we hold the little bags of bones, it seems futile, but even after the first night the bunnies look better. By the second night, a few of them are hopping around the basement floor.

Later that week, Greta makes several calls to the local wildlife rehabilitators:

Karen: "Oh, I'm sorry, but I don't do rabbits. Try Jill."

Jill: "Karen said I do rabbits? *Ha ha ha.* You might try Sue."

Sue: "Jill had you call *me*?" Sue then explains to Greta that we should make a nice cozy corner somewhere for the rabbits and try raising them ourselves. Greta, thinking quickly, explains to her that we *would* if we didn't have these two large—*really LARGE*—hunting dogs who, in another week or two, will be chasing bunnies full time. And, she explains, since the dogs live in the house with us, there will be no way to ensure the little rabbits' safety. There's barely a pause as Sue tells us her address and to come right over with the rabbits.

Sitting in the car, I watch the sun set as Greta and the girls take the bunnies into the woman's house. I'm amazed as a crow lands on the roof of the modest ranch-style house, walking down the rain gutter and peering over as it looks in the side window.

One of her former clients, I guess.

The author hunting squirrel.

There are also several ducks, a pair of pigeons, a goose, and two seagulls walking around together in the backyard, picking here and there at the ground. It is like an escaped flock from The Island of Misfit Toys.

September 12—Squirrels

"Get one, Dad?" I ask quietly into the radio.
No answer.
Walking briskly through the woods in the direction of the shot, I suddenly see something from beneath the brim of my hat. Racing hell-bent through the leafy treetops, a gray squirrel is shaking branches and raining down beechnuts. It's heading straight for me. In one of those magically detached moments, the kind I associate more with archery or pheasant hunting, my shotgun brushes gently into my shoulder, as if guided by a hand other than my own, and fires. The motion is smooth and familiar,

My father searching the treetops for squirrel.

the recoil from the .410 merely a nudge. Before my brain catches up with the action, the fat bushytail is at my feet.

When I hold it up by the tail, its depthless black eyes are level with mine. Looking into them briefly, I see nothing there but my own reflection. I silently tuck the warm critter into the game pouch, absorbing its waning body heat into my lower back.

When I find Dad, he's fixated on a young oak with his head pointed toward the sky. "I think he's in this one," he says, not even turning toward me.

"No, I think I got him," I say, reaching for the proof in my game bag.

"No, not this one. He's still here."

Walking around the tree with heads up, we stalk. Around and around the tree we go, trading places, following each other, eyes never off the treetop, as if we were performing some ancient, tribal, tree-worshiping dance.

"I've got him. On the trunk," Dad says, stopping.

Rounding the tree, I stand by his side, trying to follow the barrel of his shotgun up into the high branches. So many knots protrude from the trunk, so many little deformities that could be a squirrel's head . . . I don't see it.

"Go around," he says, lifting his shotgun.

Not taking my eyes off the area where Dad is certain the bushytail is, I move. When he shoots, the squirrel just materializes in midair. Dad smiles as he tucks it into my game pouch. Glimpsing another squirrel running between two trees at the edge of the field, I walk slowly that way.

At dusk, the sun dips to the horizon unencumbered by cloud cover and the fields radiate in its last warm glow. Sitting just inside the woods against a hickory, I face out toward the decimated pond, the one on which I'd hung all my goose season hopes. Around me, the hardwoods stand guard—the massive white oaks, the plentiful red oaks with their delicate limbs, the beeches, the hickory, a handful of black walnuts. Looking out once again on the broken pond, I can't help

Chasing after these guys is one of my favorite ways to spend the day.

pondering the fate of this rich mix of hardwoods and the little plot of land that has been their home for centuries. The woods are under the same hardhanded ownership as the pond, and I'm afraid the fate of the woodlot may already be sealed. The riches I find in here—the deer, the turkeys, the bushys—are no match for the cold cash this timber is worth. Magic has never won out over money. For now, though, the strength, the concrete solidity of the hickory where my back rests, reaches through me and makes me believe that it may just outlive another generation or two. It might provide cover and food for a hundred more generations of squirrels, providing a hundred more years of good hunting for the lucky people who know where to look.

As night settles in on the woods, the crickets and frogs begin their serenade. Once again it feels like summer.

September 15—Success

I fall asleep waiting for the sun to come up. Time is lost.

Finally waking to the sight and smell of Ted, who's also asleep with his huge black head resting on my stomach, I lie still for a moment, not wanting to disturb his sleep. Then, realizing how bright the sky is, I sit up. Teddy lets out an annoyed groan. The sun's already been up for a few minutes. Halfway down the field, John is rearranging a few decoys. The bright sun quickly warms the stubble field. Walking back toward me, looking over the decoys, John adjusts the head on one here, turning a body there. He shakes his head as he approaches.

"That first bunch should've been here by now. They've been as regular as clockwork this week."

As he speaks, John has his back to the west. Over his shoulder, I see motion. Five geese crest the woods at the opposite end of the field. I try to tell John several things: one, "Get down"; two, "Geese are coming"; three, "Turn around"; four . . . well, four didn't really matter. It all comes out something like this: "*J-J-J-Get-Geese-down!*"

Laughing maddeningly at me, he thinks I'm doing my impression of a dim-witted friend of ours, but today the dimwit is me. I thrust my index finger over his shoulder and he just says, "Get outa here, you jerk."

Then he hears the honking. Diving for the cover of the netting, he realizes his gun isn't loaded. Seeing John's movement, the geese flare straight upward, severely altering their course to the north. They're about twice as far out as the birds we missed the other day and I hesitate to take the shot. Pulling the trigger at the last minute, I frantically work the pump, firing twice. One of the geese tumbles out of the sky, hitting the soft earth with a loud *thud*. Ted races out and pounces on the dead bird, pinning it to the ground with his front paws. Cocking his head to one side, he obviously remembers his first goose, waiting to see if this one's going to try and get up. As I'm jogging toward Ted, John suddenly hisses, "Get down!" The four remaining geese are passing over my head, and this time I'm the one with the empty gun. John takes a shot, but the geese are already climbing quickly and escape untouched.

I curse myself for rushing out of the blind too soon, but the dead goose in my hand gives me a feeling of pure satisfaction. Ted makes some high-flying leaps to get at the bird as I hold it up to show John. Finally convinced he's not going to get his paws on it, he races insanely around the field, knocking over half the shell decoys in celebration. There's fire in his eyes as he charges each decoy, flipping them skyward with a lightning fast sweep of his neck

I don't bother to scold him, and it takes only a few minutes to reset the toppled deeks. My heart is still pounding with excitement, and I feel like running around the field, too. With the last of the decoys uprighted, I glimpse motion down by the blind. John is waving madly at me.

Here they come!

September 17—Desperation

Curled up against my left leg, Ted drools on the knee of my waders. I scratch the soft black fur between his ears, and he lifts his head to maximize the effect. He's almost a year old now and has been fairly easy to train, but I've not yet seen him in real action. He did all right in the goose field, but water retrieves are different. I got Ted not only to hunt in this vast swamp, but also to retrieve ducks in the unpredictable waters of the upper Niagara River. A poorly trained dog can mean a lot more than lost ducks. It can mean a dead dog. More than one hunter has watched helplessly as his retriever was swept down the river, unwilling to give up. Niagara Falls has never been known for its forgiveness.

Today I'm anxious to get Ted on a true water retrieve. The geese may be unwieldy on land, but in the water the dog should be able to bring one in. We've practiced on Lake Ontario, shooting 12-gauge blanks and using *huge* retrieving dummies. At first he'd been hesitant about the deep water, but after a few short days, he plowed water like a bulldozer. Actually *diving* off the rocks, he'd fly six feet out over the water, splashing down and paddling hard. For some of our training sessions, I brought Maggie and let her retrieve while Ted watched from his tether. When he was finally set free, his enthusiasm was cranked up several notches. When both dogs swam for the dummy, Ted easily outswam Mag with powerful strokes of his muscular front legs. Finally, there was something Ted could whip Maggie at, and he enjoyed proving it.

Today could be his true test, though. I don't know how deep this part of the swamp is. I just know that ten yards off the man-made bank the water is deeper than the top of my waders. If I drop a goose out there, it will be up to Ted to bring it in. A dozen shell decoys stand guard behind me on the bank; two are poked in at the water's edge and two floaters bob in the water just ten yards out. Fifteen yards to the left of the floating decoys, I set two pairs of wood ducks on a whim. Getting the floaters out was an adventure. I'd stood in the squishy-bottomed swamp, tying anchors to decoys by the light of my penlight and standing chest deep in the opaque water. I was surprised when Ted appeared at my side. He merely swam up, checked out the two floaters, gave me a quick sniff and swam back in.

The goose music is strong out in the dark. It sounds like a thousand geese. To my right, on a small island in the swamp, a great horned owl hoots his guttural, "*Who cooks for you? Who cooks for you?*" The sound is fitting here in the darkness.

As specks of light begin gathering, struggling to multiply on themselves and form a tenuous strand of daylight, one of the bigger flocks of geese picks up. Their excitement and purpose are apparent in the volume of their honking. The flock, a hundred birds or more, is high—far too high—but the sight of the geese flying beneath the cloudy pink canopy is truly beautiful. Ted sits up, head all the way back, his attention focused on the honkers. Sensing me watching him, he spares me a brief glance, quickly looking back to the sky, then back to me, then the sky again. He's asking me, "You *do* see those geese, right?" He watches the flock vanish in the distance.

The faint red light quickly dies from the sky as daylight reveals its true color to be slate gray. The flock, a moment ago huge, is now merely a group of specks headed north to the great cut cornfields lining the Lake Ontario shoreline. Some might meet with gunfire there, but most will return after dark tonight, mixing their music with that of the ducks and blending it with the owl's low cry and the peeps of a few frogs, to replay the dark symphony I heard this morning.

When the wind picks up, the sky suddenly seems full of ducks. Two big flocks of mallards swing over my shoulder and touch down on the other side of the pool, hidden from my view by the small island. A moment later, a dozen wood ducks circle the pool, locking and unlocking their wings, hesitating. At the last moment, they all flare, save for one, and fly off. The single hen drops in next to the goose deeks and paddles her way to the four wood duck decoys. Spotting the duck immediately, Ted is half launched before I collar and wrestle him onto my lap. The commotion doesn't seem to bother the hen, as she eyes each of the four plastic ducks. Not happy with the decoys' silent company, she swims to the bank, stopping at the end of my submerged feet.

Shuddering with excitement, Ted stirs on my lap, but stays.

Suddenly realizing something is amiss, the hen lifts loudly to the sky, followed by Ted's deep "*woof!*"

Hearing the honking before I do, Ted cocks his head, snapping to attention. I look at him questioningly, and then I hear it, too. It's coming from behind the island where all the mallards went. It might be only one bird, but the sound is the urgent, distinctive call of geese coming off the water. I spot them—three of them—as they round the golden leaves of the half-submerged aspens on the island. Banking sharply, they head right at me. My heart pounds as my stomach goes in two directions at once. Leveling off, they fly perfectly parallel to the swamp's edge. No longer honking, they promise to fly right over us. Something makes them flare away at the last second. Swinging the heavy long-barreled Winchester, I put the lead goose behind my bead and pull the trigger. There's no doubt about the hit. Feathers fly. The goose drops hard, landing just the other side of the floating decoys. Water sprays high at the impact. Seeing no motion from the goose, I command Ted to "Fetch!" Leaping over our gear, through the cattails he hits the swamp hard, sending a wall of water out in front.

That's when the problems start. Unexpectedly springing to life as Ted hits the water, the goose—whose head was hanging limply beneath the surface—comes up fast. What do I do? There's no time to decide. All the stories about wounded geese drowning dogs flash through my head as Ted closes the distance. Attacking fast, the goose slaps the water next to him like the final stroke in a hard-fought arm-wrestling contest. That's all it takes.

"Ted! Come! Leave it!"

Ted goes in for another grab, and the serpentine head almost connects this time.

"LEAVE! LEAVE! LEAVE!" I try to keep my stern command tone, but it's no use, and I realize I'm screaming. The goose sways, its head leaning sickly to one side—*maybe it's finished*—then pops back up again, full of fight. I can't believe it.

The dog hesitates only a second longer before swimming back to me. As he gets closer—and far enough away from the goose—I rain three more shots down on the wildly flailing bird. Each shot circles the goose in a tight, deadly ring of BB shot. After the ripples settle, I feel sick. Picking up a piece of rotted wood, I heave it toward the goose. It splashes down a few feet to its right. Nothing. Not a twitch.

"OK, Ted." I don't even get "fetch" out, and Ted is on his way, eagerly snorting as he approaches the goose, but something is wrong. Ted's getting farther out, *and so is the goose.* The damn bird is still alive and swimming farther into the swamp, neck down. It's heading right for an acrewide island of cattails. Ted hesitates, looking back to me. "Go on! Fetch," I holler, gambling that the bird's fight is mostly gone. With the water already to the top of my waders, I get as close to the action as I can.

Turning back without second-guessing me, Ted closes on the bird. But with only ten feet between the bird and the shelter of the cattails, he isn't fast enough. The goose disappears into the cattails with my dog right behind it. There is much splashing as I catch glimpses of Teddy at the edge of the cattails. Then nothing. Suddenly I spy the goose sneaking along the outside edge of the little cattail island.

Pouring over the top of my waders, the swamp water runs down my chest and around my waist. Holding my gun high, I walk deeper into the murky water. The swamp tops my waders by three inches, but the muck beneath my feet is still relatively stable. I'm halfway out to the cattail patch, and the water is up to my neck. About to turn around, I sense a slight decrease in the depth of the water. I'm not thinking about the hunting license pinned to my back, now a foot under water. Luckily, the floor of the swamp comes up quickly. In a moment, it's so shallow only my knees are submerged. My waders didn't seem full as I crossed the swamp, and I thought the tight-fitting neoprene might have kept all but the sneakiest water out. Not so. As I exit the deep water, the waders balloon around me, holding gallons and gallons of water against my skin. Leaning over, I unhook the chest straps, draining out a startling amount of swamp. Rushing to my side, Ted quickly checks me out, then dashes back into the weeds.

Where could the goose have gone? Slogging across the swamp, I was watching carefully but hadn't seen it come out. The only way it could not still be in the island of weeds is if it headed out the back away from me. There's nothing but open water out there and Ted most likely would've seen it go. Searching the foot deep water, Ted probes every inch of cover and looks behind every cattail as I stay on the edge to see if the goose sneaks back out. Splashing and crashing around inside the nearly impenetrable weed bed, Ted works his nose furiously. Each time he pops out of the weeds, I motion him back with a sweep of my arm and a "get in there!"

Now that I'm up in the wind, my legs start to chill. I'm shivering as I realize something that should have been obvious when the water started running down my chest—*this is stupid.*

I'm shivering more violently now—not a good sign, considering the air is fairly warm. Not wishing to turn the tragedy of the lost goose into a case of hypothermia, I whistle for Ted as I slosh back into the brown water. My spread of decoys on the bank seems awfully far away. Ted paddles along slowly next to me, although he could reach the blind in less than a minute if he wanted to. I'm grateful for his company. I'm only waist-deep when I step on a submerged branch and stumble, going face first into the smelly swamp water. My gun— fairly dry until now—is shoved forward and under the surface as I struggle to keep my balance. Wiping the duckweed out of my eyes, I push on, following what I think is the right course.

It isn't. With one tentative step, I sense the nothingness below me. Catching myself, I stagger backward, away from the unseen hole. Plowing into me from behind, Ted crawls up my back. Having swum for the better part of an hour, he must think that my shoulders are as good a place as any to rest. Now chin-deep in the water, I grunt, pushing the eighty-pound dog off me. Tasting the septic flavor of the swamp as it floods into my mouth, I nearly vomit.

A red pickup roars by on the access road near my blind. A guy looks out at me with binoculars. Unbelievably, the truck quickly revs and takes off, not caring to see whether I make it.

John and Ted in the goose swamp with one of my hunting partners.

This is hell.

Removed from my back, Ted has run out of patience, and he quickly swims across the pool to the blind. I'm thinking about losing the waders and trying to swim, too. It's a bad idea that I quickly dismiss. As I carefully feel my way around the hole, the soft muck begins to give way to shallower water. I'm relieved when it is only up to the top of my waders. Ted is already sitting in the blind, watching me intently.

Grabbing the decoys on the way in, I see two geese fly over me, circling the cattails as they strain their necks, honking down into the weeds. Their calls aren't answered. I envision the goose lying dead in the weeds. Ted could have passed within a few feet of it and not seen it. The geese circle once more, finally landing on the far side in the open swamp. Maybe they have spotted their partner.

I feel horrible, absolutely sick.

Apparently rested, Ted dives into the swamp, angling toward the island. I don't blame him but whistle him back and put him in the truck.

Shucking my waders and socks, I notice the soaked hunting license and that triggers another thought: My wallet. Reaching into the back pocket of my soaked hunting pants, I feel for it. The wallet has an oblong and slimy feel. As I take it out, it's nothing but a lump of leather and paper. In the rearview, I see Ted looking out the window toward the swamp. I see the sense of unfinished business in his big, drooping eyes. He worked hard today and all we have to show for it is some soaked hunting equipment and a lost goose. I let him curl up next to me on the front seat and his warmth feels good against my soaked legs.

"That's the last time we come here without the canoe, boy."

Looking up at me he sighs, his puppy eyes looking old.

In the afternoon, I'm still kicking myself over the lost goose. It's too hard to concentrate on the work that should be done around the house, so I take Maggie squirrel hunting. For the past few years, she and I have been the hunting team, inseparable partners. Now she has to adjust to the fact we've taken on another player. Whining and crying at the front window when I leave without her, she doesn't seem to understand. I can't help wondering what would have happened if Maggie had been in the swamp with me this morning. I never would have been able to call her off the wounded goose as I did Ted. She is unstoppable. Either she or the bird would have ended up dead, and I would not have put money on the goose.

The day draws to a quiet close after its windy, tumultuous life. The big beech trees overhead hold onto some bright green leaves, and they stand out in stark contrast to the gray sky. Sitting attentively next to me, Maggie watches the woods. She sees the squirrel before I do. I try to get a grip on her as she lets out a subsonic growl, but it's too late. Rushing the big gray, she nearly catches it as it flings itself onto the smooth gray bark of the nearest beech tree.

The woods are beautiful. The rain pouring in through the canopy makes a mute hiss as it hits the leaves. Still sitting against a tree, I raise the little pump shotgun and wait. Maggie stands at the base of the trunk looking straight up, searching, one paw lifted slightly—a tree point. Suddenly scampering around my side of the tree, the squirrel sneaks a peak around at Mag. When it climbs out onto a big limb to get a better look down at this strange brown and white fox, I ease off the safety. When nothing but the top of its head is showing, I pull the trigger. Tumbling out of the tree, it nearly lands in Maggie's waiting mouth. Pouncing on it, she watches it for a moment. I think she's disappointed the chase has gone out of the little critter. Follow-up shots are rarely necessary with Maggie around. Gently picking up the squirrel, she trots over to me and drops it in my lap. Seeing the proud look on her face as I slide it into my game bag takes away some of the residual anger still haunting me from this morning. Wagging her stub, Maggie is happy as hell just to be here. I'm happy too, but part of me is still back in the swamp. I close my eyes and—not for the last time today—see the goose disappearing into the cattails.

September 19—The Swamp

There is no wind this morning, and the starlight is dazzling. The owl once again hoots on the island, but this time his low calls are nearly drowned out by the goose music and the duck songs. Out in the dark, it sounds much different than it did two days ago. The honking and quacking are nonstop. I don't know if it's the sudden cool snap following the storm of the past two days, but something has the creatures on edge. The entire swamp sounds alive. The stars shine brightly here, well away from the suburban lights. I think of the night in the mountains with Howard not so long ago, when we were counting satellites and contemplating the

Setting goose decoys on the swamp. It won't be long now. . . .

34

coming season. It was only a month ago, but on this cool morning, the warmth of that summer night seems more distant.

An hour after daylight, the geese haven't yet picked up. The sun shines brightly and the sky is deep blue. Unbelievably, two hunters start setting up a blind only a hundred yards from John and me. How did *they* know that the geese weren't going to fly until later this morning? They are still stretching their blind material between two stakes when five geese fly over, a little too high for a shot. Something makes the geese drop suddenly, perhaps some unseen decoys the other hunters have set. Locking their wings, they dive straight for the unfinished blind. For a moment the geese appear to be hovering, looking straight down into the other hunters' laps. One of the geese unexpectedly crumples and drops, practically on top of them. A second later the shot's report reaches us.

An hour later the successful goose hunters are already gone. They had no dog, weren't wearing waders, didn't have a boat, and somehow managed not only to drop a goose but to drop it onto dry land. Thinking of the treacherous swim for my wounded goose, I silently curse them. But once they've gone, we have the pool to ourselves. Paddling quietly, I steer the canoe around the island where I lost the goose. At the cattail clump I get out, tying the canoe to the tall reeds. The place is much less forbidding today. Wading around in the long swamp grass, I hope to find the dead goose, just to close the case. But there's no such luck. I spook a pair of coots and they flush wildly to the sky. It's not surprising we didn't find the goose in here. I was almost standing on top of the little birds before they flew. For all I know, the goose might still be in here, circling me.

Back in the blind, John complains about the fair weather. Restless as always, he takes Ted for a walk to do some scouting for duck season. He's only fifty yards from the blind when a lone goose shoots over the levee. He shoots, missing it cleanly. His cursing is not lost in the breeze. The bird was headed straight for our blind.

Around ten, we have to go. Carrying one bag of decoys to his car, John is suddenly yelling to me. I see the two honkers just as they crest the levee. Reaching for my gun—still loaded but resting on the pile of blind mesh—I quickly remove the safety and swing after the second bird. The shot feels good, but the geese aren't touched. There isn't time for a second shot before they pass out of range.

Just before dark we return to the swamp, setting out only a handful of decoys before hiding ourselves and Ted in a clump of cattails. The air has warmed considerably since this morning and the mosquitoes are thick. Sweat trickles down our foreheads. The bugs and the heat would be more tolerable if anything were flying, but the sky is empty and we wait in vain.

We're packing up ten minutes after legal shooting light when Ted suddenly snaps to attention. John and I follow his gaze. Even though we are on the levee, silhouetted against the darkening sky, two geese fly straight at us just over the water. There's enough light to shoot for the next fifteen minutes, but there is no government forgiveness in a public hunting area. John and I have already unloaded our guns.

Ted runs down to meet the birds at the edge of the swamp. Flaring at the water's edge, the geese soar over John, passing just a few feet above his head. They're so close I'm surprised they don't hit him. Finally seeing us, the birds climb quickly. He follows them with the barrel of his old Browning. Turning toward me, he's wearing a big grin when a shotgun roars twice behind us. We watch as one of the birds plummets to earth, not far from the road.

John is pissed. "See, that's what I mean," he says, somewhat obliquely. "That's what I hate about public hunting areas."

"So let's go get their license numbers," I suggest, forgetting for a moment that John is actually crazy enough to confront armed people. As we're leaving, what has transpired becomes more clear. The guys had been loading up their trucks, but their guns were still loaded. One had simply grabbed his gun, taking a few potshots at the high-flying geese. *Of course* he dropped one of them. This kind of guy always does.

When I pull my truck next to theirs, John rolls down his window.

"Nice shooting," John says gruffly to the two scruffy-looking characters by the truck.

"Oh, I don't think we got it," the younger one says sheepishly and looks at the other—maybe his father—for guidance. He's obviously lying to us. The other won't meet his eye, turning back to whatever he is messing with in the bed of the old pickup. It dawns on me that they're probably going to wait until well after dark to retrieve the goose, not wishing to be noticed by a game warden. I want to leave before our conversation escalates into something nasty, stepping on the gas just as John starts to say something else.

Good timing.

John rowing across the swamp after the morning hunt.

September 25—The Last Goose Hunt

Dawn breaks early on this clear, warm morning in the swamp. Not even the thinnest cloud cover breaks up the sky, which seems to stretch forever. I'm thankful the mosquitoes are dormant. With the warm temperature, I expected them to be terrible. Maybe they are finally done for the year. Sitting attentively next to me, Ted watches each duck and redwing blackbird with great interest as they pass in the day's first gray light. It's as if he knows this is our last goose hunt of the year and, like me, wants to soak up every sight, every sound.

A few small groups of geese have already checked us out, but they wouldn't come close enough for a shot. John suggests we spread the last few decoys out a little farther, thinking they are too concentrated around us. Sounds reasonable to me. After tying Ted's leash to some cattails, I climb up the dike. Our two floaters in the duckweed have been joined by a pair of coots. I never saw them come in. They are prehistoric-looking with their bright beaks and furlike feathers. Walking down to the last two decoys, I pull them off their metal stakes. Suddenly Ted is at my side, leash dragging and tail wagging. I wondered how long that would take.

"Joel!"

Ripping the shotgun off my shoulder, I have my finger in the trigger guard before I even look. Spinning around, I see John kneeling and looking out over the water. In the dim first moments of light, it's hard to spot the silent geese. Only a foot off the water, they're coming straight at us. I wonder if they're planning to land in our decoys. If they do, they'll splash right down in front of me. Ted sits quietly now at my side, watching the geese come. I kneel down as they rapidly close the distance, racing their reflections across the dark water. The click as I push in the safety makes Ted adjust his weight excitedly.

Slowing over the decoys, the geese spot something—perhaps the odd silhouettes John and I cast against the sky—and flare up. John and I are fifty or sixty yards apart as the geese sail between us. We shoot as one and the geese are caught in our crossfire. I hoped all three would come down, but am still thrilled when the lead gander folds and crashes into the swampy pool behind us, making a tremendous splash and sending spray up over the tops of the cattails. In the midst of the action I manage to reach down and unsnap Ted's leash, sensing that, if I had done it a second later, my fingers might have left along with Ted. He crashes out through the first wall of cattails and into the murky water. A moment later he's coming back.

Without the goose.

Envisioning a wounded goose in this tangle of weeds causes a familiar panic. John is closest to where the goose went down and he quickly crashes into the water, sternly yelling for Ted to follow. We are right behind him. Inside the cattails, the pool is no more than sixty feet long and ten feet across, but the goose is nowhere to be seen. John fights through another wall of cattails that opens up on another pool. I'm in up to the top of my waders and can't take another step when I hear John again.

"OK," he says, his voice different now, calmer. "Fetch Ted!"

Ted swims past him, struggling briefly in the weeds. His big black head is covered with gobs of green duckweed. I stand back and wait. "Good Boy! *Good* Ted!" John is cheering. Ted breaks through the second weed wall, swimming right to me. Steering the warm goose into my chest, he nearly knocks me backward.

John slaps me on the shoulder and takes the goose to look at it, saying, "Ted'll be all right, I think." I can see behind his eyes that he's thinking about his Lab, Mike, now gone six months. Mike, who hunted the river with him for years. Mike, who swam in the treacherous currents, not giving up on ducks most dogs wouldn't even *start* after. Mike, whose last year was his best year in many. He'd sit stoically in front of our blind up on the river, calmly watching over the water. He couldn't see well anymore and his hearing was gone, but the spirit was still there. One night after a hunt last winter, Mike just left and never came back.

For the next few hours nothing comes in to the decoys, but there are more geese in the sky today than we've seen all season. The early morning warmth gives way to a north wind, sending a chill through me. Just before twilight, my dad joins us in the swamp. Honking and quacking of every sort serenades us into the evening. The cool breeze has turned cold. The big migratory flocks will soon be arriving in earnest, and in a short time, everything will change. The loose, small groups of ducks and geese we've been watching for weeks will be replaced by organized V-shaped flocks of hundreds of geese and countless squadrons of mallards and wood ducks. The millions of wing beats that carry the birds here will simply drive summer away, forcing it to the south, where it will be welcome for a little longer. Summer, now only a few days absent, seems to have been gone forever. For the first time this year, I feel that the last outpost of the off-season has been passed.

The wait is almost over.

For now, the local ducks and geese do their best to fill the air with music, waiting for the others' arrival. As the sad and joyous songs of autumn play into the ruby sky, I lean into Ted, stealing some of his warmth. For the first time in months, I truly feel alive.

Into the Season

October 1—Woodcock

The afternoon rivals the summer's dreams of how it would be. Gold tinges the field, the green having been ever so slightly tarnished by two early frosts. The ground isn't too wet, though we've had a few days of rain this past few weeks. The dogs, fresh from summer training, are quick to the whistle, working close. The woodlots at the edge of the big field are also colored from the frosts. Most of the trees are green, but the ones facing north are splashed with red and orange. The old brush pants and hunting vest feel comfortable and familiar against my skin even though they've been hanging in the musty basement, ignored for more than half a year. Dad's old Stevens side-by-side is slung over his arm, and my new Stoeger is held at the ready across my chest. I've been swinging it at imaginary birds for weeks, waiting impatiently for this moment.

Racing around the golden field, Maggie and Ted dart in and out of the fifteen-foot-high poplar saplings. For a moment, it seems I'll have to whistle to move Maggie along. She's got her nose buried in a small mound in the middle of a clump of grass. Not acting birdy, she's just sniffing around when a woodcock launches from under her paws.

"*Peepeepeepeepeep*" it cries, flushing to the sky, darting wildly in midair as I struggle to get the shotgun up. Its flight is so erratic that it changes direction a dozen times before I find the front trigger and fire. By the time I find the second, the bird is out of range, whistling off into one of the thick hedgerows.

Next to me, Dad says, "I think it landed in that tree in the corner."

"What?"

Sure enough, the woodcock is sitting in the top of a maple tree, its fat silhouette outlined against the sky. As I take a few more steps trying to get in range, it flies off into the next field. Still looking up into the tree, Dad appears as if he's not at all sure what he just saw.

Working down through the field, we push farther and farther into the saplings. Maggie snorts in front of me, suddenly birdy. Her motions quickly switch from casual quartering to reckless bounding. Ted, only a few feet behind, is also a completely different animal. His shoulder blades are jagged angles, pumping up and down like pistons as he works the same scent trail. Snorting like a barnyard pig, his nose drags the ground. It's been so long since

One of my hunting partners, Ken, in a patch of woodcock cover.

I've seen Maggie birdy; I barely remember what to do. Clearly Maggie isn't about to slow down, and I quickly run up behind her. Dad is still behind me, so I motion him to get out ahead of the dogs. Just as he starts moving, Ted turns from Maggie's side, rushing straight at me. The hen pheasant flushes right at my face, then quickly banks over Dad's head. Locking its wings, it coasts out over a mowed path, touching down in the adjoining field. Maggie stops in her tracks and sits, watching the bird.

Ted, on the other hand, has exited the field, rushing headlong into the next one. Not wanting to take the excitement out of his first pheasant flush, but also not wanting him to ruin the next field for us, I whistle him back. Stopping short, he looks back at me, hesitating. I can almost see the devil on his shoulder, begging him to chase the bird. I whistle again, and he takes a quick look over his shoulder where the bird landed, finally bounding back to me, tail wagging.

"Good boy!"

Just before dark the scarlet sky casts a picture-perfect hue over the bird fields. My neighbor's dilapidated old barn displays a familiar silhouette on the horizon as we turn back toward my house. Dad and I are talking when the next woodcock flushes, and, although we get the guns up, it quickly drops back to the field. Neither of us has time for a shot. It lands only fifty or sixty yards away, so I give the dogs the signal to "get in there, get in there." Woodcock are usually easy to coax into repeat flushing, and I'm surprised when this one isn't. Normally they don't land in trees, either.

I'm so sure we are just missing the bird that I send the dogs through the little patch of cover three more times. Working every inch of it, they eventually get bored. No bird. Near the end of the field, Maggie again snorts in the long grass. The errant hen pheasant takes wing, flying back where we first flushed her.

At home the filthy dogs flop on the cool kitchen floor. Seed pods and briars fall off them in clumps. Exhausted, they sleep for two days.

October 3—Two, Alone

Upland hunting is a social sport. There's always someone who wants to come work the dogs with me. I enjoy that dimension of the hunt: the company, the endless chiding over missed shots, the running bets on who is going to be the first one to fall face first in the field. There's always plenty of laughter. There are also the times when I'm out there alone, except for my silent hunting partners—the dogs. I treasure these days the most.

Maggie and Ted course steadily back and forth in front of me. On most days Ted trots along on Mag's heels, relying on *her* nose to make the first find, but today he's working the field in perfect counterbalance to her. Maggie crosses from right to left, Ted from left to right. They each range out forty yards before crisply turning back and crossing again. The wind in our faces keeps the dogs working close. Turning back down the field with the wind at her back, Maggie ranges farther. Cutting back toward me, she tries to get her nose into the wind. This is when she'll usually flush something just out of range. There is a fine line between too close and too far, but for now she's quartering perfectly.

The sunlight warms my back, though the day doesn't plan to get much above the freezing mark. Watching the dogs run the golden field, it's too easy to forget I have to work this afternoon. The morning begs me to stay, though I should be sleeping.

Suddenly locking up, Maggie shifts to her left, peering into an outhouse-sized clump of dogwood. Pulling the glove off my right hand with my teeth, I let my finger settle into the trigger guard. Ted, coming from downwind, immediately picks up the bird scent and dives into the clump. The woodcock flutters from Ted's side of the brush. The shot from my 20-gauge seems distant. Feathers fly as the woodcock arcs over the field, landing in another dogwood patch. Ted, as graceless as ever, crashes in behind it and I hear him sniffing. For a moment I wonder if the shot was good, but I stop worrying when Ted emerges with the bird. His head is so big that the woodcock looks like a chickadee in his jaws. Delivering it to my outstretched hand, he pauses right on cue to receive his "good boy." Maggie appears at my side, placing her paws on my brush pants to stand up and smell the warm bird. I ruffle her ears as she takes in the aroma of her bird.

Such moments are what I'll be dreaming of six months from now.

The next woodcock is almost an afterthought. Reaching my neighbor's barn, I break open the 20-gauge and start to unload it. Looking once more at my watch, I decide another half-hour can be spared in good conscience. The sky is now crystal blue, the field awash in the polarized light of autumn, and the dogs are still working beautifully. Such days are not made for getting to work early. They're made for this.

A rabbit zips out from under my feet in the poplar saplings but I'm distracted by the dogs. By the time I see it, it's halfway gone. I'm not quick enough. I consider bringing Maggie around and putting her on the scent, but I don't wish the final push of the day to end in a joyride through the countryside after a rabbit, when we know there are at least a few more birds in this field. I decide to keep the sighting to myself. Ted is suddenly bounding around madly, and I wonder if the rabbit ran his way. At the same time, Maggie is birdy at the edge of the field. I try to watch both dogs—each intent on something, but forty yards apart. The woodcock flushes behind Maggie, and I feel awkwardly slow as I lift the gun, spinning to the right. Somehow the bird either flies intentionally into the shot pattern—committing suicide—or I just shoot well. Later on when I tell Greta, I'll claim the latter, suspecting the former.

On the way back to the house, the dogs heel quietly on either side of me, though I haven't asked them to. They're tired. Walking along, I don't think about the workday rapidly approaching, but about the fact that perhaps I'm not such a bad wing-shot after all. Of course, nobody was here to see it but Maggie and Ted.

Today, their approval is all I need.

October 7—Phil

I wasn't hungry this morning, perfectly content with a few cups of coffee. But ever since setting foot into the field at seven, Phil has talked nonstop about the upcoming game dinner at his sportsmen's club. He described the venison at great length. He went on about the antelope, spoke mountains about moose meat, babbled about the buffalo, and jabbered about the jerky. It seems last year's game dinner was fantastic, and this one promises to be even tastier. My stomach is rumbling uncontrollably now and I'm about ready to hit him. *Hard.*

Over the next hour, three hens flush from the long grass. One of them circles the field twice before flying across the road where our trucks are parked. Around nine, a large flock of Canada geese picks up off Bond's Lake, a mile up the ridge. Splitting into two groups, the flock hugs the escarpment, then turns northwest into the wind. Their honking is getting louder, as if every bird in both groups is talking at once. Taking off my hat, I stretch my neck to see the two separate Vs.

"Joel, look at Ted," Phil says.

Ted is sitting quietly in the grass, his head swiveling, alternately watching the geese and me. Phil starts laughing.

"He knows what they are, I guess."

"Yeah, he's seen a few of them."

Just for fun, I raise the shotgun and watch Ted out of the corner of my eye. As the gun goes up, so does his rear end—-ever so slightly—before settling back to the ground. When I suddenly swing the gun to the right, up comes his rear again. His mouth is opening and closing, drool flowing freely. I can't stifle a giggle as he fixes intently on my every move.

"Good boy, Teddy. Go on now and get the birds." After I sweep my arm out with the "go on" sign, he sits a moment longer, making sure I don't want to shoot at the retreating geese. Every now and then, he takes a break from the cover to search the sky. Phil asks how we did during goose season, finally switching the subject away from the food I now desperately crave.

When a woodcock flushes unexpectedly out of a tangle of old grape wire and vineyard posts, we are still talking about geese, but the guns come up quickly and we both follow the bird as it wings over the dogs' heads. When our shotguns roar at the same time and the bird falls, I am surprised. I'm not surprised at the woodcock. The place is loaded with them. I'm surprised Phil didn't beat me to the shot. He must be out of practice. Last year, Phil hunted with me almost every time I went for pheasants. His speed and accuracy were constants. If I missed a rooster, he would drop it. If one flushed in front of him, it never made it to me. He was hell on the rabbits, too. He came along as a guest of one of my pals, Brian, on last year's pheasant opener. His easygoing way and sense of humor made me take an instant liking to him. The fact he was out of work made it easy for him to join me on the hunts I squeezed into my odd schedule. I don't mind having someone who can *hit* birds as a hunting partner, even if it does make me look worse.

Once last year, Maggie flushed a huge rooster that we all missed. Watching where it went down, we decided to follow it.

We ran Maggie along the little hedgerow where it went, but she turned up nothing. The only spot she missed was a fallen limb lying out into the grass field. The unmowed spot around it created a bathtub-sized patch of cover. It looked perfect and we all knew the bird would be under it. Right before I sent Maggie in, Phil said, "You get the first shot. If you miss, I'm taking it."

The bird burst out right on cue as Maggie dove under the branch. I've never shot so fast. The rooster didn't go more than five yards. Looking over my shoulder, I saw Phil laughing, his gun still on his shoulder.

"You didn't have to shoot *that* quick. I would have given you another second or two."

"Bull," I told him, letting him know I saw him putting his safety back on.

Twenty years from now, if I remember one thing about Phil, though, it won't be his wingshooting. It will be the day Phil and Brian and I went gray squirrel hunting in Ransomville—my hometown.

It was January, long after ringneck season had closed. That sunny winter day Phil sealed his lifetime membership in our little hunting crew. We'd managed to strafe the top of the oaks enough to bring down one fat bushytail. Not seeing anything else, we decided to cross a drainage ditch to the next small patch of hardwoods. The ditch had a few inches of water in it and was four feet deep and five or six across. It didn't look like a hard jump but with my bulky hunting clothes on I knew I was an accident waiting to happen. I watched closely as Brian, who's a foot taller than I, leapt over the trench. On the way across, several of his shotshells fell down into the mud. Seeing him barely span the gap, grabbing a sapling to keep his footing, I said, "No way." Lowering myself down the steep side of the trench, I quickly stepped across the muck at the bottom. Brian held out a hand to help me up the opposite bank. Then Phil, who is about my height and a few pounds heavier than I, flung himself out over open space. He made it halfway.

When Phil disappeared off our radar, we ran down the ditch to see if he was OK. Lying on his back in the muck, he looked up at us with a dopey grin that suggested he had just discovered he couldn't fly. Brian, always quick to quip, asked politely, "Hey Phil, while you're down there, could you please pick up my shells?" At this, all three of us started laughing hysterically. Phil climbed up the bank, pulling himself up on the exposed roots and not getting much help from Brian and me, still in stitches. When Phil finally joined us again, he just shook his head, still smiling. Brian and I made it across bone-dry, but not Phil. Coated in mud from his head to his boots, he shook his head slowly at us, unable to remove his sheepish grin. Brian and I were still laughing when Phil bent over to do something. Whether it was to wipe the mud off of his pants or fix his boots, I don't know. Somehow, he lost his balance and tripped forward. The top of his head smacked squarely into the trunk of a huge oak tree and the impact resonated through the quiet woods. Racing for Phil, we caught him before he could fall. Later on, Brian would tell me he was afraid the impact had killed him. I was thinking the same thing. It was *that* loud.

After sitting dazed against the trunk of the tree for a few minutes, though, Phil was ready to go. Brian and I told him he should have his head looked at by a doctor. Already sporting a sizable goose egg, he would have none of it. The three of us hunted quietly back toward the road, but every now and then one of us, usually Brian or I, would simply go into a laughing fit. It was irrepressible. It was contagious.

The scene of Phil's fall—followed by his head-on with the tree trunk—was simply so humorous it refused to stop playing in my mind. Brian was having the same problem. We shot another squirrel, though how we did it through our laughter is beyond me. After we killed it, it hung up in the upper branches, precariously balanced. Brian suggested Phil use his head and "ram the tree until the squirrel falls out." This time, the tears streamed down our faces as we laughed. Before we left the woods, I took a picture of Phil and Brian holding up the two bushytails. In the picture, Phil's eyes are markedly unfocused and his hunting hat is hanging from his head at an unnatural angle. A year later, I still can't look at that picture without bursting into laughter.

When Ted brings me the woodcock, I give it to Phil. He enjoys cooking, particularly when it comes to wild game. For a moment I'm not thinking of my own hunger, when off he goes again about this dish and that dish.

"OK, Phil. Let's go get breakfast."

"Thought you'd never ask."

October 11—Hens, Running

Only here an hour, Dad and I are getting worn-out already. It seems like every time we turn around, one of the dogs gets birdy. The problem (though not a big one) is that all the birds we are flushing are pheasants. We haven't seen a single woodcock. I don't mind running around a field and chasing my dogs as they pursue a rooster; strangely enough, all of our runners today have been hens. The hens that ran on us last year could be counted on one hand. In this spot the runners were always roosters. If this is how these hens are going to act with the dogs on them, I can't wait to see what the roosters will do.

When they have flushed their fourth hen after a hair-raising chase around a small pond, it's all I can do to call the dogs off. My ears ring from the whistle as I blow the long tones meaning I want the dogs back now. The whistle also bothers a cottontail that managed to stay hidden at the toe of my boots. I take a fleeting shot as it zigzags off through the grass, untouched by my hasty shooting. The shot brings Maggie and Ted back quickly. Charging back up the field, they pick up the scent. Making a snorting beeline through the grass, Maggie runs straight to a pile of discarded vineyard posts. With both dogs circling the pile like sharks, I can only imagine what the rabbit must be thinking.

The air is damp and, although it's not too cold out, a chill comes over me. My kids have been sick all week, and if I survive this month without ending up in bed, it will be a miracle. The sudden absence of the woodcock doesn't surprise me. The season used to open on the first of September, and we saw a lot more birds. Now that it opens in October, I think the local population has headed south and the good shooting happens only when a flock passes through. Those days are few and far between in October.

Back near the truck, I point the dogs into a small patch of cattails near the road. When the state stocks pheasants, they invariably drop a few right there. Ted has just entered the reeds when a fat rooster slowly takes flight, hovering before flying clumsily past us. Dad follows him with his shotgun.

"Even I could have hit him," he says with a broad grin as the rooster sails across the field. "How long till bird season?"

My heart is pounding. The flight of the rooster has sent me two weeks into the future. "It's right around the corner."

October 12—Ducks, at a Distance . . .

The cadence of John and Ted snoring in the cab of my truck may be familiar, but it does nothing to facilitate my own plans for rest. Giving up, I walk down to the dark shoreline and sit on a boulder. Ted must have whined for John to let him out because soon he is at my side, huddling against my leg, quickly falling back asleep with his head on my lap.

The Toronto skyline—yesterday just a silver mirage—is now a thing of beauty. It's hard to imagine, sitting here in the middle of the expansive shoreline farmlands, that such a grand metropolis is merely a boat ride away. The lights from the CN Tower and the surrounding skyscrapers cast a warm orange glow into the black night, and the entire city basks in a fiery aura. East of downtown Toronto, the lights get lower and lower into the suburbs, finally trailing off into the occasional speck of light here or there. I imagine those single splashes of light are floodlights on barns and streetlights of small towns, the welcome signs on greasy diners, and the headlights on the cars and trucks of people up early leaving for their jobs. I wonder what they are dreaming of and hoping for this calm morning. Are their dreams any different from mine?

An hour later, the truck dome light winks on and I hear John shuffling around in the back. Racing around, Ted is well rested as I help John unload the decoys and boat. There's no good spot to put in on this rocky shore, so we merely bump the boat down over the boulders, finding a fairly level place to get it in the water.

I pull on my old, patched waders and familiar duties are quickly delegated. Rowing his boat out, John will set the bluebill decoys while I wade out and set the mallards. Same as last year, same as always. John will arrange the bluebills fifty yards off the shore in a nice tight group, and I'll set the mallards in loose formation along the shoreline.

Wading out ten yards, I rig my mallard decoys. It seems that every anchor cord is tangled. Farther offshore, John's flashlight beam bounces crazily out over the glassy water as he struggles with his own mess of tangled lines and uncooperative plastic ducks. The sky brightens quickly and unexpectedly. Hollering, John asks how the two dozen decoys look. They look fine, but he doesn't seem to think so. Yelling again, he asks me to get the handful of remaining decoys that are still lying in back of my truck. After fetching them I wade out to the boat, dragging the decoys out in a ragged line behind me. I'm surprised at how level and firm the lake bottom is all the way.

"Careful, these took a lot of anchor line to set. There's probably a drop-off here somewhere," John is cautioning.

Luckily, I listen to him. I'm in just over waistdeep when the bottom gives way. Backpedaling fast, I manage not to slip at the edge of the drop-off. I feel the lip of the drop as I regain my composure, gathering up the decoys I let go. The lake's water is still warm and I wasn't overly concerned about falling in. After my day alone in the goose swamp, I'll never be scared of filling my waders again.

Ducks over Lake Ontario. As usual, they're just out of range. . . .

By the time the sun turns the sky from gray to blue and has picked itself up over the glassy water, we have already seen many hundreds of ducks. Several flocks of buffleheads and goldeneyes, a few stray mallards, and a smallish flight of canvasbacks all passed us, flying from east to west. The problem is that the ducks are all hundreds of yards out from shore. *Hundreds and hundreds and hundreds* of yards.

The goldeneyes are easy to pick out, even though they're too far away for us to hear the distinctive whistling of their wings. The sunlight catches their vivid black-and-white coloration with each of their hurried wing beats. Several woodies also pass, flying along the shoreline until reaching our blind, then swinging wide over the lake or passing behind us on shore. They either see our blind or are just instinctively avoiding the point. The most plentiful birds on the lake today, as always, are the buffleheads. From a distance, they resemble the goldeneyes, though only about half their size. The drake bufflehead rivals the goldeneye for its beauty. Its large crested head sports a pompom of white, making it look far too big for its tiny body. Sitting on the water, the male bufflehead is a regal sight. Above the water, the goldeneyes fly in tight groups, moving swiftly about ten feet off the surface. The buffleheads fly the same speed as the bigger ducks but tightly skim the water's surface, even when flying in groups of a hundred or more. On windy days, they disappear between the wave troughs. The buffleheads also have a knack for flying right at the horizon line. Even on calm days like today we're probably seeing less than half of the birds.

Our problem is that none of the diving ducks show even the slightest inclination of swerving into shore to check out our decoys. Unlike mallards and woodies, the divers can't be lured in with a call, so we sit helplessly silent as raft after raft of bird passes us out of range. I'm surprised we haven't seen any bluebills yet.

Smaller than mallards and slightly larger than woodies, they taste remarkably like mallards—surprising, given their fishy diet.

My mind returns to a day last year when the sky was blue like this and the sun was beating down on us. We did very well, and it was with bluebills. It was around Christmas and the weather had been miserable and cold for two weeks. The hunting on the Niagara River had been steady, and we'd brought home ducks each time we went. The bluebills were flying well. Though not close, at least they weren't on the Canadian side, as they had been earlier in the morning. Their flight always amazes me. Flying in tight flocks, they match one another wing beat for wing beat, banking and turning in unison. Unlike the other ducks, which always have stragglers, the bluebills move as a single, tightly orchestrated unit. They move precisely, like a school of fish. Sitting there basking in the sunlight, we watched chunks of ice drifting hurriedly down the powerful river. Jay's black Lab, Jake, was curled up on his rug next to me. A flock of bluebills a hundred yards out suddenly banked toward us. We all nearly fell over in surprise, quickly scrambling for the guns. Jake sat up, noting our excitement and watching the ducks come in. Unlike the ducks that taunted us all morning, this flock of thirty or so veered straight for our decoys. They set their wings over the decoys in unison, hovering for a magical second above the water.

At the roar of the guns, six bluebills splashed into the water. Jake was off like a rocket. As he approached the first duck—the one nearest to shore—it dived and was never seen again. There were so many chunks of ice floating around that it may have popped up anywhere and we simply didn't see him. Swimming in frantic circles, Jake searched for the duck that had evaded his jaws by mere inches. Jay hurriedly pointed him to the next duck, which he quickly set on the shelf ice in front of the blind before grabbing

Ted exhibiting his usual enthusiasm for duck hunting.

one of the two that had fallen into the decoys. He came back carrying the second duck and dragging one of the decoy ropes, with two decoys attached. When he started struggling in the ropes, I was the only one with waders on. I hustled.

Splashing quickly out into the water, I untangled Jake's front leg from the line, taking the duck from his mouth and tossing it to Jay on the bank. I picked the other duck out of the decoys and gave it to Jake, who carried it in to Jay. There were two more ducks, now already several dozen yards downriver, riding with their legs in the air. I pointed one of them out to Jake who simply couldn't spot it mixed in with the ice chunks. Jay threw a rock at the duck to mark it for the dog. Jake swam too far upriver from the duck, missing it. In frustration, he retrieved a piece of ice. I tried wading down to the rapidly drifting ducks, but even the closest one was in neck-deep water. The Niagara River is no place to swim in January. Luckily, at the last minute Jake spotted the

56

closer duck and, paddling hard, got his mouth around it and dragged it to me. Stuffing it down the front of my waders, I searched the water. The last duck was barely visible downriver. I didn't realize how far we'd already gone until I saw Jay running along the bank behind me.

"Forget it. It's too far," he was yelling. "It's almost to the next blind—let them get it."

The current caught the bank at an angle and was surprisingly strong as I fought to get back to the shelf ice. At the edge of the boulder-strewn bank, the water was up to my chest. I was nervous as I tried to pull myself up. Next to me Jake—already tired from his long swim in the cold current—whimpered as he struggled to climb out on the ice.

With his front legs splayed at an awkward angle, he cried, trying to pull himself up. Twice he slipped back, going completely under the frigid water. I quickly waded over to him and tried to give him a boost by holding his collar but didn't have enough leverage.

Yes, we finally managed to hit one.

Struggling harder, Jake panicked. Reaching underwater, I grabbed the base of his tail, heaving him up on the shelf. Jay looked relieved as Jake rushed to his side. I wasn't so relieved. I knew if the dog couldn't do it, there was no way I was going to. Pulling the duck out of the front of my waders, I tossed it to Jay. I resigned myself to walking back up against the current to the shallower water near the blind. The walk against the river was hard but I took my time. When I reached the blind, Jay was on the bank to give me a hand up on the ice. The sun still shone fiercely, but the right sleeve of my coat had frozen solid. I'd taken only a few steps on the slippery shelf ice before I lost my footing, falling squarely on my face. The arm I threw up trying to stop my fall would hurt for days. Taking a moment to compose myself, I looked downriver and my breath caught in my chest when I realized how far I had gone—and how foolish I'd been.

A few minutes later, a game warden arrived. A familiar fixture on the public blinds, he came and sat with us. Checking our guns and sifting through our pile, he told us we were the most successful group he'd seen today. Suddenly ducking down, he pointed out a small group of bluebills headed right at our decoys. Jay and I shot, dropping one of the birds, which Jake eagerly dove in and retrieved. As the big dog swam in, already recovered from our downstream fiasco, I thought to myself, "I *have* to get a black Lab." Hence Ted.

We killed a few more ducks that sunny morning—buffleheads—and dividing the duck pile at noon, we all agreed it was the best day we'd had yet. That day was a far cry from today.

The decoys haven't drawn in a single duck. At nine, several strange-looking birds suddenly appear in the water to the east of the blind. They seem to be swimming our way.

"What the hell are they?" John asks.

"You're the duck hunter," I say to John, who gives me a dirty look.

"They're not canvasbacks—too low in the water," he says, thinking aloud. "They could be loons, but they look a little too small. Not mergansers, too low again."

"If they're eiders, you can shoot 'em."

"How do eiders ride in the water?"

"Don't remember exactly."

Great.

John paddling the creek for ducks.

October 13—The Creek

The canoe moves silently up the creek. The only noise is the occasional muted thump of the paddle against the hull. John sits in the bow, his shotgun lying across his lap. The green-winged teal we shot this morning is at my feet on the floor of the canoe, looking like a midget next to the mallard decoys. Of the several ducks that checked out our decoys, this was the only one that came in. After our long day on the lake without a shot yesterday, this tiny duck was a welcome sight.

Duck season is not getting off to a great start.

On our way in this morning, we saw a few guys in blinds on the creek bank. Each of the groups was friendly and said the same predictable thing, "You should have been here yesterday." Every one of the guys we talked to shot ducks while we were sightseeing on the lake.

Of course.

Today the ducks are wary from yesterday's shooting, and we kick ourselves again. For months we had planned to come here on opening day, only to change plans at the last minute. "Next year," we tell ourselves, "next year . . ."

The birds were still flying when we picked up the decoys an hour ago, but they had avoided us, flying to the far side of a bend in the creek. We watched where several landed and decided to paddle out to try to jump them. There were a few hairy moments paddling through the upper branches of two fallen trees. The branches gently bumped the canoe beneath us, and with our luck, I was sure at any moment we'd hit a big one and capsize.

In the narrower part of the creek, the bottom quickly becomes visible. John points out a swirl on top of the water, and I paddle toward it. A huge brown trout—seven or eight pounds—shoots under the canoe, disappearing into the deep water behind us. As John turns back to the front, seven wood ducks erupt from a tangle of willow roots. When he picks up his shotgun, I stop paddling. The canoe glides forward. I see the six hens and a drake over his shoulder as he follows them with the barrel. The birds are silhouetted against the branches that overhang the shady creek. The branches are silhouetted against the blue sky. Faint light dapples the gravelly creek bottom. The colors of the drake are radiant, bathed in autumn light. The moment is frozen.

This is hunting.

The Heart of the Season

The valley holds memories, and deer.
The deer thrive in the valley,
I thrive on the memories.
At times we meet.

October 14—The Keys to Paradise

I can't believe we're here.

Contemplating this place and time in the long months leading up until now, it seemed so far away. It was nearly untouchable. Sitting on the old rail fence and basking in the afternoon sunshine, we look out over the Catskills and off into Pennsylvania. I know we're here and that it's real. Finished hanging our tree stands, we wander the property, checking out all the familiar spots; I guess you could call it "scouting," but it's really much less formal than all that. Like reintroducing yourself to an old friend, it's not necessary, merely polite. As I do every year, I feel I've been handed the keys to paradise.

The farm is four hundred acres of hardwoods and pine ridges, hemlock bottoms, and tiny, spring-fed trout brooks. The abandoned orchard that once served as a home for cattle and then horses is now home only to the wildlife; the red and gray squirrels, the turkeys and coyotes, the foxes, hawks and owls . . . and the deer. They come to the orchard—now only a dozen or so scrubby trees that have gone wild—to eat the small, bitter apples that fall to the ground. My paradise is full of deer. Their trails, used by generation after generation, are etched deeply into the landscape. Every year there are new ones, but the old ones never go out of use. Some of the traditional trails are so rutted into the landscape that during times of heavy rain they become rivers coursing down the hillsides.

Doc, the landowner, is out of town this week, and I'm disappointed. A retired surgeon from New York, he is one of the most pleasant people I know. Always taking time to share a story, he's never without kind words for my wife and her family. Greta's grandfather used to be the caretaker here. He laid many of the stone walls and dug out the holes for the rail fence where we sit, watching a dozen deer feed in the open hayfield in the bright sunshine. As a result of his long hours and tireless labor up here, we now have the right to hunt the property. His sweat—along with Doc's generosity—has given me this place, this outdoorsman's heaven in which to play. I shot my first squirrel here, as well as my first deer, my first coyote, and my first grouse. Having hunted here only ten short years, I've already buried a large chunk of my heart in these rocky hillsides.

In another month, the farm will resound with the voices and laughter from the rest of our hunting crew, but my dad and I are the only bow hunters, and we have this lovely chunk of mountainous beauty all to ourselves. There isn't one single moment that I'll forget what a blessing I've been given.

Not for a second.

October 15—More Blessings

When dawn breaks over the orchard, I've already been in the big hemlock tree for a half-hour. I shiver in the dark, as much from anticipation as from the temperature. The hemlock, my home for the next week (and for many weeks over the past years), pokes my back with a single lumpy protrusion, keeping me from getting too comfortable. I don't mind, though. I have no desire to fall asleep. Not today.

A few moments before shooting light, a fawn enters the orchard above me, crawling under the rusty old barbed wire fence separating the field and the orchard. Coming closer, it's silhouetted perfectly against the gray-blue sky of first light. It crunches noisily

The white-tailed buck, bigger in my dreams than in the woods. . . .

across the frost-laden leaves, not following the trail but cutting straight through the narrow strip of hardwoods. It's on a direct course for the apple tree ten yards to my left. Passing two other apple trees on the way, it doesn't stop, knowing this one has the most fruit. The ground around the base of the tree is littered with fallen apples, most of them half-chewed. I knew yesterday, when I leaned my weather-beaten ladder against the hemlock, that this place was once again the best place in the orchard. The trails leading to this tree are so entrenched in the meadow grass, they look as if they have been dug with a shovel. This tree has always been a charm for me. I took my first deer only a few yards from it and killed my last two bucks while hiding in its branches. The lump on the trunk of the tree, now poking more insistently at my back as I try to sink into the cover of the limbs, is merely a familiar, if uncomfortable, reminder that I'm in the right place.

As the deer approaches the apples, I can see two fuzzy little nubs on its head. The button-buck pauses ever so slightly when it crosses the path I walked on this morning. Its wheels turn as it contemplates this strange smell. An experienced doe or a buck might have bolted at the smell of a human this far back in the woods, but this young deer seems not to remember even having noticed the scent. It passes only two feet from my ladder. Quickly engrossing itself in the plentiful apples, it eats below me while I hold my breath. Heart pounding at an alarming rate, I enjoy the first close encounter of the season.

Every year it's the same: The youngest bucks come to feed early, sometimes before daylight, then exit the orchard before the does with fawns arrive. The older bucks come in after them. The youngsters seem to know through obsperience that the other deer will chase them away from the apples. Consequently, they've learned to eat quickly. When I first hunted here, Doc kept his horses in the orchard. I was uncomfortable hunting with them nearby, but he insisted I hunt there because the deer were bothering his horses. Without too much arm-twisting, I obliged. What I saw amazed me. Every two hours, like clockwork, the horses made their rounds through the orchard, picking up whatever apples had dropped to the soft ground. When the horses spotted a group of deer, they charged them. Chasing them off, they wouldn't stop until the deer were driven all the way over the old wire fence surrounding the orchard. Standing at the fence, the horses would whinny and snort at the deer until they disappeared into the creek bottom. An hour or so later, the deer would sneak back into the meadow. Standing at the edge of the orchard, they'd look back and forth—like pedestrians in the city watching for buses—until they were sure the horses weren't around. Hurrying to the apple trees, they'd quickly gobble apples before the horses' inevitable return.

I managed to arrow a buck that year. We decided the quickest way to drag it would be back through the orchard and out to my truck parked on the side hill. As Greta carried my bow and pack and I dragged the deer, one of the big mares walked up behind us, suspiciously eyeing the dead buck. Horses always spook me, and when this one started snorting and rolling its eyes, walking right along behind us, I began to worry. The mare lunged threateningly at the deer, slamming its frying pan-sized hoof into the ground only a few inches from the buck, only three feet behind me. I was sure at any second the horse would slam its foot down on the deer and pulverize it. With my arm caught in the drag rope, I'd get turned into hamburger, too. I've never dragged so fast in my life. It's but one of a thousand memories that have been made here in the quiet valley.

The button-buck still below me suddenly freezes. It's caught wind of me. Its eye is the only part of its body that moves. It seems to be looking under me. Moving stiffly, the buck walks out from under the apple tree, stopping thirty yards in front of me.

As it turns broadside, I see the apple hanging out of its mouth. In another moment the deer relaxes again, and I clearly hear the *chomp chomp* as it finishes the apple. Without warning it turns and trots away, disappearing into the shade of the hemlocks below the orchard. Staring downhill into the dark creek bottom, I try to spot it. So engrossed in seeing where the little buck went, I barely notice the three deer that entered the orchard from my right. I'm about to stand and stretch when a white antler in the bright sunshine catches my eye.

My rear end, only slightly raised, slams rather unceremoniously back onto the seat. The buck is sixty yards out, and there are two other deer with it. Both have their heads buried in the long meadow grass. The buck is a large six- or seven-pointer. Looking around, it casts only casual glances in my direction. Leaving the company of the other two deer, it walks toward an apple tree, crossing the old overgrown pathway and giving me a good look. Watching deer moving calmly and carelessly like this in the early season is one of the things that draws me here year after year.

The deer's dark coat shimmers in the sunlight as it turns this way and that, trying to vacuum up the apples before its companions get to them. The other two deer slowly move toward the tree, casually browsing on the grass.

The first of the two to cross the path is a small spike-horn. Grabbing my binoculars, I doublecheck. It's tiny. The last buck remains a mystery for another minute or two. Since it's turned broadside, its body size is hard to judge at this distance. I'm watching it through the binoculars when something makes the deer snap its head up. I nearly fall out of the tree. It is a monster. Its bone-white antlers are thick and wide, their bases looking like tree trunks. My heart pounds as it calmly looks around, finally burying its head back in the grass. Resuming its slow grazing pace, it's still heading steadily in the direction of the apple tree.

When the deer crosses the path, I get a glimpse of its body. The animal is huge. Its legs are fully six inches longer than the six-pointer's. Its chest is deep and its coat thick and dark. Fattened on these apples all summer, it is in prime shape heading into the November rut. It joins the other two deer under the apple tree, but they pay no attention. In two weeks, when the rut starts, the buck won't tolerate their inferior presence, but for now they share the apples in perfect harmony. I helplessly watch the three of them feeding peacefully eighty yards away. Rather than try to call them in with my grunt, I'll wait to see where they plan to go next. If undisturbed, they may walk around, checking every tree in the orchard. There are so many apples on the ground around them right where they are, though, that I doubt they will do this. My suspicions are proved correct when, after ten minutes of feeding, the three deer head into the cover of the hemlocks. With his fat rear end pointed at me, the big buck looks like a moose. It's almost twice as wide as the six-pointer.

Quickly taking the grunt call out of my shirt pocket I let go with a loud *"errrrrrrrp."*

The effect is instantaneous, even at a hundred yards. The little spike quickens its pace, disappearing over the knoll into the hemlocks. The two bigger bucks stop dead in their tracks, each looking in a different direction. They're unsure where the sound came from. Gambling with having my location pinpointed, I grunt again while their heads are up.

Both deer wheel around, looking directly at me. With the bucks up a slight incline from me, I pray I'm high enough not to be spotted. Trying to sink back and melt into the tree, I feel exposed. The six-pointer snaps its head back and forth, looking behind, then looking toward me. It pauses again and then turns, walking calmly back to the shelter of the hemlocks. The big buck still hasn't moved. Experience has probably taught it just to freeze, letting the intruder show himself. Rooted in place, it displays none of the spookiness of the six-pointer. It wants to know who this strange buck in his territory is, his body language unequivocally stating that he's the boss around here. If this had been the rut, I'll bet the deer would have charged across the orchard to drive off the would-be trespasser.

Now it just stares.

With a slight cock of its head, it suddenly looks right at me.

I usually don't panic too badly in such situations, but there is only so much preparation for this. Not moving is tough. My own body is my worst enemy. Every inch of it suddenly itches, begging me to scratch. My rear end is pleading to be shifted on the rigid metal seat. The hair caught under the brim of my hat is insisting I pull it out. The bead of sweat running down my cheek urges me to wipe it away. I try to ignore them and stay still. All it will take is one little movement, one twitch, and this buck will be history.

Still it watches.

Realizing I'm holding my breath, I try to let it out gently. Instead it comes out ragged and harsh, seemingly sending a tremor across the whole mountain range. I'm sure the buck has sensed my breathing, but it hasn't moved. I'm amazed it hasn't heard my heart beating. I can actually hear the blood flow like a raging river in my ears. My eyes water slightly, feeling like they're bugging out of my head. *This is buck fever.* Without any warning the buck breaks into a trot. With head held high, it rushes toward me. Closing the gap to fifty yards, it stops dead again next to a woodpile. From its new vantage point, it seems disoriented, having lost my exact location. It looks slightly confused.

Perfect. Calming down, I mentally prepare to shoot.

Turning its head in all directions, the buck searches for the intruder. All I need is twenty yards. Just a few steps and it'll be in range. I don't dare touch the grunt call again or the deer will look right at me. As is so often the case, I now have to rely solely on luck. Today it proves unreliable.

Pivoting on its front legs, the buck makes a hard right-hand turn, pausing for a few seconds before walking into the hemlocks. The pause would have provided a perfect opportunity for the shot if it had only been fifteen or twenty yards closer, but at fifty yards, there was no way. Just as the deer enters the shady edge of the creek bottom, I let go again with a loud grunt. There is a slight hitch in its step, but it pretends not to hear, heading into the dark woods. Despite the missed opportunity, I'm smiling. Three bucks in the first few hours of the first day—this is going to be a good week.

For the next hour, I remain rock-still in the tree stand. I've hunted this spot enough to know that one or more of the bucks I saw are circling around the orchard, concealed in the dark woods, watching and smelling for the creature that made the noise. Every now and then, I catch a glimpse of white and brown as an ear flickers or a tail twitches down in the timber. Every inch of my body is suffering from muscle cramps. Even my fingers throb. They've been wrapped around the bow grip in the exact same position for over an hour now. My neck is cramped from not moving and my eyes are suffering the strain of trying to see in every direction. It's been at least half an hour since I sensed any activity down there. I'm famished, having rushed out of the house with no breakfast and not enough coffee. Reaching around for my pack, I feel a sense of dread. Before I get the zipper open, I know I've left my lunch at the truck. With six more hours until sunset, starvation is not an option. Again reaching for the binoculars, I carefully scan the woods. Nothing. I'd planned to hunt all day, but since it's only the first morning, I don't feel too guilt-ridden as I climb down.

The walk back to the truck is steep but takes no more than ten minutes. I move slowly so I won't spook any deer that may be watching. I'd been thinking about just grabbing my lunch and my thermos and heading back to the stand but decide instead to take a break and relax for a bit. The sky is beautiful and the air has an autumnal crispness to it. How many times, deep in the warm belly of summer, have I dreamed of such days? Nearing the truck, I wonder how my dad is doing but don't have to wait long to find out. He's getting out of the front seat. Just finishing a lunch break himself, he's had a slow morning. A single doe passed his stand at daybreak but was too far out. As I dig for my sandwiches and coffee, he's preparing to head back to the stand.

"Remember, give me two beeps if you get one and need help," I remind him.

Sandwich in hand, I open the front door of the truck to get in, then have an idea. Why don't I hike up the driveway the rest of the way to Doc's house and have lunch on his back porch? I'll have the scenery of the hills to enjoy while I eat. Rounding up my hunting equipment—so I won't have to come back for it— and my lunch, I quickly walk to the house and make myself at home on the weathered picnic table on the back porch. The view is spectacular. To the right, several apple trees line Doc's side yard. Beyond them, the valley we're hunting and beyond that a breathtaking view of the Catskills. On this clear, deep-blue day I can see well into the hills of Pennsylvania. Off the back porch, a huge hayfield stretches to a thick spruce-covered hillside. It's the same field we were watching deer in yesterday. It isn't uncommon in the evening to sit here and watch a dozen deer feeding on clover and grass. The apple trees in the yard are usually raided after dark, and the side lawn is covered with deer droppings. Many of the ornamental trees and plants around the house have been eaten, rubbed, and otherwise ravaged over the years. There's no shortage of deer here.

Staring off across the field, I'm lost in thought when a young spike buck appears at the edge of the pines, hopping the barbed wire fence bordering the field. Two hundred yards from me, it steps into the field at high noon. With a healthy piece of sandwich hanging from my gaping disbelieving mouth, I can't believe it!

After looking down at my bow, lying in the grass next to the driveway, I sense more movement. Two more deer, both small bucks, join the other. Quickly raising my binoculars, I note the second deer is also a spike, but with only one antler. The third is a fork-horn with ridiculously small headgear but a huge, fat body. It stands nearly a foot taller than the two spikes. I rise from the

Whitetails in the morning mist—a sight I dream about all year long.

picnic table carefully and slowly, but all three bucks detect me, staring. They quickly dismiss me, probably used to seeing people moving around the house. I drop to my hands and knees, below the level of the old stone fence that separates the backyard from the open field. Peeking over at them, I watch the bucks feeding slowly across the field. Looking toward the big pond about five hundred yards from Doc's house, I remember the apple trees. They are absolutely loaded with fruit this year. Could that be where the bucks are headed? Not during the middle of the day. They could just as easily have stayed in the woods, skirting the field to get to the more secluded apple trees in the orchard. Why would they cross in a wide-open space? I peek over the fence again, and—sure enough—that's where the deer seem to be headed.

Crawling toward the two low spots in the fence—the traditional crossing places for the deer—I periodically peek over the fence at the bucks. They've stalled, feeding on the grass in the center of the field again. Quickly scrambling another twenty yards, I peek. Crawling another fifty, I peek again. I've covered a good distance when the deer suddenly turn, looking back toward the pines. Have they smelled me? Did they hear me? Are they getting ready to bolt for cover?

As the bucks and I watch, a doe and fawn emerge from the pines. Realizing the sound is from the other deer, the bucks resume feeding. I'm sweating profusely and my knees are sore from crawling. The arrows in my quiver are rattling loose from repeatedly slamming against the ground. I can't decide what to do. In another fifty yards I'll be at the old gate, one of the deer crossings. Another hundred yards will put me at a broken-down part of the fence the deer also use as a crossing. If I go to the first opening, the wind will be at my back if the deer decide to cross there. That would be bad. If I continue to the second opening, I can get downwind and hide in a couple of small spruce trees, but it will also mean crossing the first opening and taking a chance that the deer will spot me. I opt for the second opening. The wind will be right. The trees will offer some concealment, and this spot is farther back in the field, out of sight of the house. If I were a deer, that's where I'd cross.

Without any time to think about the downside of this shaky plan, I decide to go with it. Crawling slowly along the fence, I close the fifty yards in what's probably ten minutes but seems like an hour. The scattered maple leaves have to be avoided. Not many have fallen yet, but the crunchy, windblown piles are noisy land mines. Luckily, when I reach the old gate, the deer are all feeding with their heads down. Facing away from me, they're probably engrossed in a patch of clover. With one more quick glance at the field, I abandon my stealthy approach, scrambling as fast as I can across the six-foot-wide gap. Reaching the other side, I stay low. If any of them have spotted me moving, I don't want to further tip them off by poking my head over the fence. The fence is higher on this side and I'm able to get off my knees, while crouching low enough to stay hidden. Minutes later, when I finally do peek over the fence, I'm sure I've blown it.

It's all over.

Eighty yards away, the doe is staring right at me. Bobbing her head down as if to eat, it quickly picks it back up as it tries tricking me into moving. Whether it knows I'm here or not, it isn't coming any closer. The doe and the fawn hastily retreat toward the pines, tails bobbing in mild alarm. Fortunately, I get one more lucky break when the bucks, still engrossed in their feed, don't sense the doe's nervousness. Slowly, they continue grazing in my direction. I'm able to quickly cover the last hundred yards to the low spot in the fence, walking somewhat upright again as I enjoy the concealment of the five-foot fence. Almost to the opening, I peek over again and I'm shocked. The deer have moved right along with me and are only twenty yards away on the other side of the fence. They're headed right at me!

Dropping to my knees, I nock an arrow with suddenly shaking hands. My heart rate soars. My breathing is shallow and too fast. For the second time today, I'm fighting buck fever. I crawl toward the opening, which is now ten yards from me. Blowing parallel to the fence, the wind is at my back. It's too late to get on the other side of the opening. If the deer cross the gap, they'll immediately wind me. If by some miracle I'm given the opportunity, I'll have to shoot quickly. I don't want to shoot the spikes (especially since I saw that monster near my stand this morning), and if one of them crosses first and winds me, I'll have no chance at the bigger four-point buck.

More dilemmas.

Peeking over the fence again, I can just see the bigger deer's forked antlers. It's about ten yards from me. A few feet farther, the height of the stone fence drops down again. If the deer gets to that lower spot, I'll draw, rise, and shoot an arrow over the wall at it before it gets to the opening. A second later, the buck angles toward the gap and I draw the bow. I hold it at full draw until the deer appears broadside to me at eight yards. Quickly standing from my crouch, I place the sight pin against its chest and let the arrow go. To my horror, it sails over the buck's back and across the field. I aimed too low, and the arrow has hit the stone fence and deflected upward.

Oh no!

At the sound of the arrow ricocheting off the stone, the two spikes flee across the field. Then just one more lucky break occurs on this exceptionally lucky day: The fork-horn turns its body completely around, again broadside, looking in the direction the arrow flew. Snapping its neck around quickly, it stares after the other two bucks, confused.

Perfect.

While the deer is looking away, I manage to nock another arrow, not fumbling too badly, given the extreme circumstances. Feeling suddenly detached, I draw again and release, watching as the bright yellow fletching buries itself deep into the buck's chest. The deer doesn't hesitate, this time taking off like lightning. Watching it go, I know with certainty the fork-horn is running its last sprint, dead on its feet. Even at this distance, I can see the blood spreading across its chest. Sadness grips me as the buck gracefully leaps the old wire fence at the side of the field, disappearing into the brush. The sorrow I feel for the buck is as real as the old stone wall. The sadness is nothing new. If I ever stop feeling this way, I'll sell my hunting gear and quit forever.

Back at the truck, I try to calm my shaking hands. My appetite gone, I'm fed by pure adrenaline. When I honk the horn, I remember agreeing on two beeps. I lay on the horn for all it's worth, "*Beep beep beep beep beeeeeeeeeeeep!*" Then for good measure I do it again.

Appearing at the edge of the woods so quickly, Dad seems to have been catapulted out of his tree stand. The questions rain down on me as we climb the hill: "Buck or doe? How big? How long a shot? Where'd you hit him? Where'd he go? You were *eating on the back porch*?"

I try to relay the story the best I can, but even talking is difficult with the excitement that racks my body. I'll calm down once we find the deer, I assure myself. The walk to the field takes too long. Dad asks me if I think we should wait, but my patience is gone.

"No, he's got to be down. I saw the arrow go in at the heart."

Walking to the place I shot, I point to where the deer was standing. Dad marks the place and begins searching for blood. The thick grass in the field is a mixture of dark green and gold, and I know finding blood could prove tricky. But I'm shocked when we don't find any. Tracing the buck's path in my memory, I again walk back to where I shot. I run another straight line to where he crossed the fence. Walking up and down the fence, we don't find a single crimson drop. Staring back into the thick brush on the other side of the fence, I desperately hope to catch a glimpse of the downed deer. Nothing. My blood pressure, which had momentarily began to nose down, suddenly spikes again. Back to the open field, we quarter like bird dogs, scouring for any trace of blood. We make circles. We make grids. And we find nothing. I decide to walk the fence again. Crossing it, Dad parallels me on the other side.

It's hard to concentrate. I am overloaded with adrenaline. I feel nauseated, desperate. What if the hit wasn't as good as it looked? What if I just nicked the buck? What if I hit it in the paunch and only thought it was the chest? What if I wounded it? The tracking could take days. . . . *Stop it right now*, I tell myself. *You saw the hit. You heard the hit. It was good, even perfect. Concentrate. Look. Breathe. Sit down. Start from scratch if need be. Just think!*

"Joel," Dad says, catching me catch myself.

"Yeah?"

"Blood, right here," he says calmly, pointing at the old rusty wire.

Hurrying to his side, I immediately spot more blood in the grass—right where I'd walked before. I can't believe I missed it. Time to get my head screwed on straight. Where the deer crossed the fence is obvious. There's blood painted on some tall weeds, as well as across the wire. It's quickly apparent the blood had dripped, not sprayed. I begin questioning the accuracy of my shot again but quickly shove it to the back of my mind. It doesn't matter at this point. At least we've got a trail of blood to follow. But as I follow the blood trail back out into the field, the trail suddenly ends. All I can think is that the arrow must have stayed in the deer, plugging the wound. If I hit the deer where I *think* I hit it, the blood trail should be huge. On the other side of the fence, Dad paces up and down the overgrown logging road.

"Nothing here," he says.

"From where I was standing, it looked like he dived straight into the brush. If we don't find any blood soon," I suggest, "we'll just walk in a straight line."

Dad finds a few small drops of blood in the center of the logging road, again where I had just walked. My head is spinning and I've *got* to calm down. These latest tiny red specks are only ten yards from the wire fence and reinforce what I thought—the buck headed straight into the thick brush. Quickly following the trail through the waist-high weeds and brush, we search. Here and there on both sides of the heavily used deer trail, bright red blood has splashed the golden meadow grass. Bleeding from both sides, the deer can't be far. Reaching a distinct Y where the path splits, for a moment we don't see any blood in either direction. Then we notice why.

Where the path split, the deer elected to follow neither trail, its final leap carrying it straight into the brush. There is a bright red splash over the nearest dogwood bush beyond which I see the white of the buck's underside. Still hunched, looking for blood on the other branch of the trail, Dad looks up at me. I simply lift my finger and point. As he stands from his concentrated crouch, the deer is right there, ten yards through the brush from him. He doesn't smile, just nods. Cool waves of relief wash over both of us.

Standing over the dead buck, I feel none of the normal flush of emotions. I feel relief, pure and simple. A moment later, I'll again feel the sadness that inevitably accompanies death, but now is a time for celebration. I've hunted with guys that hoot and holler and high-five over dead deer, but I've never cared much for that. Here, in the warmth of the early season, the first deer kill of the year is heralded by silence. Dad and I quietly stand over the fallen deer. No words need to be spoken. I've no doubt what a blessing has been given to me. Not for a single second.

Myrtle and Howard

Myrtle and Howard have two driveways. One goes up to the left of the house the other, to the right. When you pull in to visit for a spell or have lunch with them—or even to make yourself at home and stay, as we are doing—you take the right-hand drive. Past the flower gardens, past the stone retaining wall, you park next to the big garage. But when you take the left-hand driveway this time of the year, it can mean only one thing.

A deer's been killed.

On the left end of the house is a smaller garage where the wood is piled high, anticipating the winter. It's where the bushels of the past summer's vegetables from a lovingly tended garden are stored, where the pulleys and ropes are, and where the few pieces of equipment needed to finalize the hunt stay until someone drives up the left-hand driveway. Just outside the little garage is a tree with three trunks. In the center of the trunks a flat board has been nailed. Originally the board was to be a platform for flowerpots, but over the past few years, the hunters adopted it as a meat-cutting shelf. More deer have hung in this tree than I can remember, and I've been doing this for only ten years. This tree has supported the spoils of the surrounding woodlands for a lot longer. Plenty of deer-hunting history has hung from its sturdy branches.

As I get out of the truck, the garage door is already opening. Greta's grandfather, Howard Sr., is ready. In his left hand, a coil of old scratchy rope. In his right, the battered pulley. On his face, a huge smile.

"Told the wife you'd get one today," he says, one crooked finger pointed at me. His face is beaming. Walking right to the tree, he

My father-in-law, Howard, in the "deer-hanging" tree.

doesn't even look in the back of the truck. Tossing the rope and pulley onto the tree shelf, he finally walks back to the truck with me. When I lower the tailgate, Howard stands with his hands on his hips. With his head cocked slightly to the side, he admires the buck. All his words are accented with excitement. It's been several years since he's been able to join us on the hill. Now his enjoyment of deer season is hearing our stories around the wood stove at night. When I started hunting, Howard still worked for Doc a few hours each day, keeping things up around the property. He could tell me where the deer were, where they weren't, and where they would be when. When we'd put on deer drives during rifle season, Howard was always a driver. He'd snake around the secret and uncivil places, often the only one of the drivers to move any deer. He called himself the "bird dog." The last few years, with him absent from our hunts, if we've come back empty-handed, he says, "See, you needed the bird dog up there."

Myrtle appears in the kitchen window above us, waving down and giving me a thumbs-up for the buck. The windowpane barely contains her wide grin. Usually, she'd be right out with us—watching us hanging the buck, giving her judgment as to the size and the potential quality of the meat—but this year her legs are worse. After years of agonizing surgery on her knees and ankles, she's long overdue for another operation, and watching her hobble around the house fills me with sadness. She's a robust woman, full of energy, opinionated. Married to Howard at sixteen, she lived a hard life of working at her family's boardinghouse, then laboring intensely on the dairy farm she and Howard bought when they first married. Their old farm—once a showplace—is long since sold, now falling to pieces. Some of the old property now makes up part of Doc's land.

Myrtle has always been the queen of our hunts. Success or not, she wants to hear every detail, every laugh, every mistake. I remember the first time I killed a deer. The weather was warm, so we couldn't leave our deer hanging in the tree overnight. We skinned and quartered, chopped and sawed into the wee hours. When the piles of meat were finally ready for trimming, it was well after midnight. The two Howards, Greta, Myrtle, and I sat at the kitchen table laboriously trimming and cutting until two in the morning. Myrtle's stories kept us entertained and laughing long past the time we all should have been in bed. Our fingers ached from the steady, meticulous knife work, but Myrtle would have none of leaving the remainder of the work till morning. Believe me, we got it done.

Hanging the deer in the tree on the side, Howard Sr. watches, wishing he could help. Thanks to a lifetime of carpentry and farming, he can't raise his arms above his shoulders, but he manages to provide me enough assistance to get the fat buck pulled up in the stubby little tree. We tie the legs to one of the smaller branches, to get them up away from the reach of any marauding dogs. My God, how many times have we done this? Exactly like this. Same branches, same pulley, same old rope. Same warnings from Howard about getting the legs high enough because of the "goddamn dogs." I could do it in my sleep. I've done it many times in my dreams.

There's always a rush after taking a deer—not the initial one but the one that comes later. The one when you want to relay every instance of the hunt to someone else. The one when you want to tell about your heart pounding out of your chest. The one when you want to tell about your eyes blurring and your chest heaving. The one when you want to tell how glad you were and how sad you were. The one when you want to brag. The one when you just want to tell it all, reliving every moment. The one that matters.

Very seldom do people have the time or the desire to listen to the telling. But when you drive up the left-hand driveway you can be sure there will be two people who'll want to hear all about it.

I wash the blood off my hands under the spigot on the side of the house where six months from now flowers of every color will be growing thick and beautiful, tended to with more care than those in any other garden in the county. Walking up the wheelchair ramp to the back door, I go in. Giving me a kiss, Myrtle points to the ham salad sandwich on the table. Kissing her cheek in return, I sit. As I dive into the sandwich, Howard comes in, taking his place next to Myrtle across the table from me. They don't say a word, but I know what they want to hear.

And I begin the telling.

October 16—Free Time

The posted signs and staple gun bulge out of the game bag on my hunting vest. Draped across my arm is my side-by. I've killed some grouse here and know the north line I'm posting is full of them. Grouse are a luxury I can't get back home. I wish I'd brought Maggie along, but who could've expected to get a buck the first day? The posted signs are in good shape this year, one or two of them needing a staple or two to get their sagging corners back up. I near a stand of young spruces separated from a stand of tall white pines by an old wire fence line. It was up here that I killed a coyote years back, the shot sending an approaching buck racing back downhill toward the drivers. Boy did I get grief from that. . . .

The narrow corridor between pines and spruce is grouse heaven and I have my shotgun ready. I can't count the times I've walked down this lane deer hunting and had grouse thunder off through the timber, scaring the hell out of me. Maggie would love it here. A grouse under one of the big pines to my left flushes toward the open lane in front of me. Sliding the safety off, I follow the bird with the barrels, waiting for the shot. To my amazement, it plops down on the trail right in front of me instead of flying across. Naturally, I swing the heavy gun right past the grounded bird. Correcting quickly, I swing back to the left. While I'm trying to put the bead on it, the bird skitters around in a crazy circle on the ground, suddenly rocketing back to where it came from. I'm left shaking my head, not quite sure what I saw.

And I thought pheasants had all the tricks.

Traveling along the fence, I stop to put a staple in one of the older posted signs. At the metallic pop of the stapler, another grouse

My Catskill hideaway.

flushes somewhere in the thick spruces to my right. Up ahead are two huge cherry trees, one that has been recently split down the middle by lightning. Under these cherry trees, there's a pile of flat rocks built up to a comfortable sitting height by consecutive years of hunters. On a side hill, the seat looks up into the Y made by the convergence of the spruces, pines, and sparse beeches lacing an open patch of fields. A small spring-fed rivulet runs over basketball-sized round rocks and down the hill next to the rock seat. Many a bloodstained hand has been washed clean in its cold water. Sitting on the pile of rocks, I lean the gun against my left leg. With the morning's frost burned off, the sun sparkles brightly on the water crystals in the open field. Beyond that, the Maple Pond shimmers in the morning sun. Beneath its polished surface, bass and pickerel cruise silently below the ripples. The clarity of the sky is glorious today, and the majestic peaks of the Catskills are visible to the north. Sitting there for a few long moments, I let the autumn sunshine warm my face. There are still patches of snow under the pines, but if the temperature stays on this steady upswing, they won't last the day. The valley below me is alive with the sounds of birds as they bask in the morning sun.

It's also alive with the memories that have been created here. The joy and the laughter, the sadness and the stress that we've experienced are all eternally trapped here, secure within the confines of the surrounding hills. The earth seems to speak, the trees to tell stories. The subtle voices that mix with the babbling of the brook are of friends, of family, of the past. There is nothing physically special about the place. It's just a few hundred acres of mountainside farmland. But the emotion that it evokes is beyond words.

Looking off into the distant hills, I feel the simple, primitive feeling of belonging. Of being home.

BIRD SEASON

Taunting from a hidden place,
The rooster knows.
In hot pursuit, the dogs know too.
The gunners, watching as the chase unfolds,
Know only what the dogs care to share.

October 20—The Pheasant Hunters

It was a long night at work, but when I get home, sleep is the last thing on my mind. Meeting me at the door, the dogs follow me around the house suspiciously since I'm not following my usual ritual of diving straight into bed. As rain splatters the windows of the dark house, I quickly fill my hunting vest with all the necessities—leashes, whistles, dog biscuits. I grab some of the jerky we made from the fork-horn, but I know it's too spicy and am hoping to pawn it off on the other guys. I wait impatiently as the coffeemaker drips and gurgles. I pull on my hunting boots and vest, the vigilant dogs still watching every move. They know the hunting clothes mean they are going somewhere, and their eyes look longingly up at me.

"Do you want to get the pheasants?"

Maggie springs in pure ecstasy, her stubby tail wagging furiously. Wiggling all over, Ted makes high jumps by the back door. He doesn't have any clue what a "pheasant" is, but hearing me ask if he wants to go "get" something is all it takes. The kitchen floor thunders under his weight as he leaps. Stepping under him, Maggie gets flattened. Her tail still wagging, she scolds him with a terse *woof*.

The dogs stay alert as the truck slices through the rain, speeding toward bird season. John's already waiting at the field. "We'll be lucky to see a bird today if the rain keeps up," he says, face sullen.

"I know."

Brian and Phil arrive a few minutes later. The walk out to the bird fields takes longer than ever. The dogs range wildly out ahead of us, and it's all I can do to keep them in sight. They are rabid with excitement. Despite the rain, so am I. I checked out the place—five fallow fields bordered by two giant cornfields—last week. It was in the same shape as last year except the cornfields had slightly shifted positions and the fields where they had been were now fallow. I found them covered with a low weed, one that looks like a miniature oak tree. The weed has a single stem branching out widely at the top, choking out the sun while keeping the grass underneath at bay. The fields of this stuff we hunted last year were full of pheasants, and their crops were full of bright green grasshoppers and corn. Maggie would get under that knee-high canopy and virtually disappear. The open ground beneath gave the pheasants plenty of room to stretch their legs and run. We managed to get several birds out of that nasty stuff, though. The corn was still standing when I was here last week, but that's OK. Last year, the corn remained uncut through all but the last few days of the season, and we still managed to coax some birds out of the surrounding fields. The few times I let the dogs run the corn, we doubled the number of flushes, but with not enough hunters to cover the escape routes, most of those birds got away. The runners played hell with Maggie in the corn.

As we round a bend into the open area, a sea of corn fills our vision. Misty rain gently hisses in the dry stalks. It's hard to keep Maggie out of the corn as we walk the length of the huge field, but I want to save her energy for the grass and weed fields and the hedgerows. I try to make the dogs heel. As we reach the end of the corn, my heart sinks.

For the first time in several years, four out of the five brushy fields have been plowed under. Where just last week golden grass and tall weeds waved in the breeze, there are now only ugly brown

Success after another hard-fought rooster hunt. The dogs have collapsed just off-camera.

gouges of earth. The furrows left by the plow are two feet deep in places. I sense the eyes turning on me.

"You checked, right?" someone asks.

"It was here last week," I say, as if the place isn't even here anymore. It might as well not be.

"The back field is OK," Brian says glumly.

That one is the smallest of the bunch, but we flushed several birds there last year. Our hopeful dreams for this place have crashed and our options are scant. We can leave and go to another area, but just walking out will take a half an hour. We could set the dogs loose in the corn—possibly not seeing them for another hour if they get on a running bird—or we can trudge across the mud to the back field where we might flush a bird or two. Finally deciding to follow a wide hedgerow to the field, we let the dogs work the thick cover of the row. We chased a few roosters up and down the length of this hedgerow last year. The row is split in two with heavy cover on the outside and a wide deer path up the middle. When spooked, the pheasants got on the deer trail and ran like mad, not flushing until the dogs were on top of them. By then, they were usually out of range. I swore I'd never put the dogs in here again. But today we are in a bind, and nearing the row, I cut the dogs loose from their heel. It's time to hunt.

They explode into the hedgerow. I catch glimpses of black as Ted slowly works the cover in front of Brian and me. John and Phil can see Maggie from their side. The field is plowed right up to the hedgerow, and walking—let alone trying to keep up with two fresh dogs in a narrow patch of cover—is murder. Each step sucks our boots down into the wet black earth. The rain pelts us harder now and there is none of the usual laughing and joking and chatter. Everyone is fighting the mud. Halfway down the field, my hips start to ache. Thankfully, the dogs work the cover slowly and thoroughly, not getting too far ahead of us. I'm surprised with this concentrated patch of cover that Maggie hasn't found some scent in here. I hope the birds aren't all in the corn. The end of the hedgerow doesn't come soon enough.

Taking a break, we hold the dogs at bay, wanting to have some kind of strategy before setting them loose in the long grass. The birds are notorious for running to the west here, not flushing until inside the heavy beech saplings at the edge of the nearby woodlot. We've shot a lot of beech branches down these past few years. Brian and John agree to stay on the edge of the trees while we work the field to the north. They'll be slightly ahead in case a runner cuts to the woods. Phil and I will work the dogs through the center of the field. We hope this works, knowing it's our only hope of getting a bird without packing up and driving someplace else. The dogs bound wildly around the field for a minute or two, just happy to be released from heel again, but quickly settle into a nice quartering pattern, occasionally swinging wide to check on John and Brian. Three-quarters of the way into the field I get a bad feeling we're not going to see any birds today. The rain comes in buckets now, soaking through our clothes, and although the temperature is around fifty, I'm getting chills. Near the end of the field, Mag finally gets birdy, feverishly bounding back and forth. Ted rapidly approaches her from the rear. He also smells it—whatever it is—and gets excited in his big lumbering way. The two dogs race a lunatic course around us in the long grass, then suddenly stop and look at us as if for guidance.

"Get 'em up, Maggie," I say hopefully, but I know she needs no encouragement. If there were something there, she'd still be working. She just looks at me, wagging her little nub of a tail. Finally turning, she calmly resumes working the field as if she'd never been birdy.

Arriving at the north edge of the field, there is a lot of head shaking and unhappy faces while the four of us brood and contemplate under the dismal sky. Just inside the woods is the drainage ditch where Phil took his tumble and knocked his head last year.

"Hey, Phil," Brian says.

"What?"

"Show us how you dive again? Please?"

With the ensuing laughter the foul mood is softened, despite the rain. Following the dogs' lead, we fruitlessly walk the other side of the field to the south, sorry when the firm grass ends and the plowed furrows begin again. The field is muddier now. On the way to the truck I point the dogs into the corn, figuring there isn't much to lose. Maybe some dumb young rooster will flush out, begging to be shot. Stranger things have happened. But the dogs want none of it.

Even muddier than the open field, the cornfield is full of long stretches of foot-deep water. The dogs quickly become disenchanted, heeling voluntarily by our sides. I feel bad for them.

"Should have gone duck hunting. I'll bet they are flying," John laments.

During the walk back to the truck, several suggestions for a course of action are floated. Chief among them, quitting.

After Coffee

The place has plenty of birds but always poses a particular problem. The fields of dogwood and old grapevines and sawgrass go on forever, but the best hunting is right near the road. The dogs dive out of the back of the truck into the cover, often making game before the guns are even loaded. So carefully getting my vest on, I find a dry hat and load my gun, the whole time taking care to block the open door of my truck with my body so the dogs don't prematurely escape. Once the other guys are ready—

completely ready—I open the back hatch of the truck. The dogs are hunting in a flash. Putting them through a patch of cattails next to the road, I hold my breath as the other guys circle the back side of the cover. I can't even count the birds and rabbits we've flushed in this patch of weeds. This time, though, the dogs appear on the far side, looking at us quizzically. Pausing only briefly, they dive into the dogwoods. Halfway down the field, it looks as if we're going to go bust again. The dogs haven't even sprung a cottontail for us. With the rain coming down in gray sheets, the ground is saturated. The whole field has at least an inch of water lying in it and six or eight inches in many places. I have no idea where the ringnecks will be. I can't imagine their finding a dry hideout on such a lousy day. Wherever they are, I'm sure they won't be very willing to leave.

John has to get to work. "When we get to the end of the field, I gotta go," he says glumly.

I don't blame him, but no sooner have the words escaped his lips then Maggie gets birdy. She's up to her knees in water, and I can't believe she can scent anything. Suddenly in high gear, she is snorting like a pig. Cutting across the field, she kicks up a plume of water as she runs. Could a pheasant be running along in that water ahead of her? *No, it has to be a rabbit.* I strain to see in the grass in front of her as she makes a straight line to the north. Whatever it is, it's right in front of us, but I can't see a thing. Wishing I could see what Maggie's seeing, I wonder if she's just following scent. Or does she see something? Is there a fat rabbit in there? Or a big pheasant, caught out in the open on this terrible day? Only Maggie knows. Suddenly stopping short, she's chest deep in water in the weeds. Eyes locked on the ground in front of her, she lunges straight back toward me, and a rooster takes flight. So sure that it was a rabbit, I'm momentarily stunned as the wet bird flies out of the puddle. John gets off the first shot, and then we both shoot. The rooster crumples in an explosion of feathers. Maggie rushes in, pouncing on it.

Yes!

Ted, who has been trying desperately to keep up with Maggie, rushes in and takes over. In a flurry of growls, Ted seizes the rooster and carries it to John's feet, dropping it. His tail wags his whole body. I forget about the rain and the cold. I forget about my soaked pants and my water-filled boots and grab Maggie and Ted. The pungent smell of wet dog fills my nose as I hug them. When the celebration finally ends, the dogs begin vacuuming the field with a new, highly charged enthusiasm. Not surprisingly, John looks at his watch and discovers that an extra half-hour or so has been added. Reaching the far end of the field, he turns—not back for his car at the road, but right along the back of the field with us. Conversation has picked up, and this gray, wet day has suddenly taken on a new feel. I've even begun to forget I haven't slept in twenty-four hours.

I'm trying to spot Maggie, who's somewhere inside the briar-choked hedgerow at the edge of the field, when Phil yells, "Look at Ted!"

Pouncing across the field to our left, Ted moves back and forth in quick jerks, his muscular flanks rippling as he blasts through the thick dogwoods. He makes no sound other than a low *sniff sniff sniff*, and there is no doubt that the boy is birdy. Branches snap as he doubles back once, pouncing again just as another rooster awkwardly flushes to the sky. The guns thunder again and the rooster crashes into the hedgerow. Maggie charges into the hedge, a moment later emerging with the wet rooster held firmly in her little jaws. Ted rushes her again, but this time she drops the bird and viciously chases him off. The snarl on her lips as Ted retreats says it all: "This one is mine." Carrying the bird to me, she gently puts it in my hand, pausing at my knee for praise. Ted rushes in to sniff at the bird—his first pheasant flush—and I hold it in front of his broad square nose as he drinks in its smell. "Good boy!" Both dogs are off again, with even more enthusiasm.

As he looks at his watch one last time, John's eyes bug out. "Holy cow, I have to go!" he says abruptly. His hasty retreat back to the road shows he wasn't kidding. Brian, Phil, and I aim the dogs—as much as they can be aimed—through the hedgerow and out into the open fields and old vineyards beyond. A rabbit races across the ruts and wires, but we don't get a clear shot. The dogs don't give it much chase, now having tasted the greater excitement of the pheasants once again. I don't know how a dog comprehends that a ringneck is of more value than a cottontail—they both can be chased, they both can be shot—but somehow they know.

Another mile is walked without a flush. The cold—having been temporarily subdued by the excitement—begins creeping back in. Coming down heavier once again, the rain suppresses the noise all around us, making conversation difficult as we trudge forward through the long grass. My hips are aching again, grinding in their sockets with each step. Brian and Phil are slowing down, too. Stopping for a moment, we discuss how much longer we're going to suffer through this rain, now much more than just a shower.

"Where's Maggie?" Phil asks.

Uh-oh.

Sitting behind us, Ted listens to the discussion, but Maggie is nowhere to be seen. I cast my arm in the direction I last saw her, and Ted races off. Stopping about twenty yards out in the tall sawgrass, he cocks his head and listens. Hearing something, he takes off on a sprint. Trotting along behind Ted, we finally catch a glimpse of Maggie seventy-five yards ahead of us. Bounding left-right, right-left, ears flopping, shoulders hunched, she's probably mere inches behind a bird. When she dashes under the first two rows of old vineyard posts and wire, I know we'll never catch her in time. We've closed the distance to her by only a few yards, and whatever she's chasing is showing no inclination to flush. By the time we could pick our way through the rusty wires and rutty trenches that the little dog is now speedily maneuvering, the bird would be long gone.

As the three of us stop, heaving and panting, a rooster pheasant takes to the air over Maggie. Winging its way over the far hedgerow, it quickly drops out of sight. As Maggie trots back to us, we marvel at the survival tactics of these wild birds. There's no way a game farm bird would know to run crosswise through the vines and then flush to the other side of the absolutely thickest, most briar-filled part of the hedgerow. This bird knew its territory. It's just one of the many huge roosters that have put us to shame over the past few years. Some guys don't want their dogs going after these runners, but if I didn't let Maggie do it, we'd rarely get any birds at all. Even the two roosters we shot this morning ran a long way before flushing.

I've hunted preserves where you can shoot twenty birds in two hours, and your ears ring from the blasts; where each bird rises from the grass with a hefty price tag dragging along on its stubby tail feathers; where the birds tend to flush straight up and taste like a barnyard chicken, which for all intents and purposes, they were an hour earlier. But this little band of pheasant hunters, an odd assortment of men and dogs, is in it for the hunt, not for the numbers. We're in it for the beauty of the trailing tail feathers of the big wild birds as they take noisily to the sky. We're in it for perhaps one bird after five or six hours of hard hunting—or maybe no birds after several days. We're in it for the thrill of an exhausted dog dropping a hard-won rooster at our feet. We're in it for other things as well, like bets on who will have the most spent shells and the least game at the end of the day. We have wagers on who will fall down first in the deep ruts. We have the laughter at our own mistakes and misses. We cherish the feel of the tired dogs' heads resting on our laps as we drink cold beers later in the afternoon, sharing more laughter when the hunt is over. We're in it for golden fields and boggy cattail patches, blue skies (sometimes they are blue) and frosty mornings. We're in it for the sudden appearance of a giant rooster where the cover says there shouldn't be room for a meadow vole. We're in it for beauty, in all its forms.

October 22—Run and Gun

Walking haltingly along the hedgerow, Brian and I know the rooster landed here yesterday. When we move slowly like this, the dogs sense we want them to search the cover thoroughly. In and out of the hedgerow—disappearing from view for moments at a time—Maggie and Teddie dust the area for evidence. Brian and I stop and the dogs come back to check on us, then rework the cover, finding nothing other than a few songbirds ("Tweety," we yell, laughing at each other for raising our guns at the fluttering little robins).

The sky is blue today, and although it's only forty now, the weatherman promised it would get into the sixties. Still wet, the grass soaks our brush pants. I can't contain a shiver as we stop at a small pond to let the dogs drink. Ted suddenly seems preoccupied with a small clump of dirt.

"Go on, Ted," I encourage him, "find the birds!"

Trotting toward me, he looks off to one side and turns back, suddenly rushing the basketball-sized dirt pile. He sniffs intently at the base of it, casually walking around the other side. Something in the grass catches his attention, and when he pounces, a small hen flushes straight over our heads. I

Ted as a puppy, jumping for Brian's rabbit.

instinctively raise the Stoeger, and the bird passes no more than a foot from the end of the double barrels.

"Hen," I yell quickly to Brian, seeing his shotgun coming up out of the corner of my eye.

"Bang," he yells back, following the retreating brown bird with his gun.

"She was history," he says. "Too bad the roosters don't flush that way."

"They do at the preserve."

"*Hrrmph.*"

The next bird takes us, like yesterday's runner, on a romp through some old grapevines. Although we're paying attention this time, the bird merely outdistances the dogs and us with speed. Running straight down a deep rut between two sets of the wicked old wires and crooked posts, it flushes fifty yards ahead of the dogs. Seeing the bird go up, the dogs start chasing it to the next field. I get a headache from the amount of whistle blowing it takes to turn them around. They want that bird badly. So do we. As we hike toward where the bird landed, my legs and hips are hurting again. I have forgotten my sunglasses, and the bright sun assaults my eyes. Even though I don't yet know the long walk will be in vain, I wouldn't stop if I did.

Late in the afternoon, the sky turns a hazy, summer blue as the temperature not only reaches the sixties but nearly stretches up to seventy. Although the sun is now on its downward trek, it's still warm for hunting. John wants to immediately work the area where he flushed and lost a rooster with Maggie last night. I let him direct the dogs into the cover. The grass is chest deep, and the slight breeze coming from the west is effectively blocked by a tall hedge of thick beech trees. Ted and Maggie both immediately pick up scent, running something straight to the hedge. Whatever the critter is, it never shows itself.

John says, "This is where the rooster went down last night."

A narrow corridor pinched between the hedgerow and a line of smaller cottonwood saplings on the edge of the grass, it looks ideal. Working the dogs up and down the corridor, we hope they'll pick up something. When John is satisfied we've searched the area enough, we hunt the field back toward the road. Maggie, just a few feet to my left, suddenly starts snorting wildly. Not bouncing around, she's moving quickly forward in fits and starts. The grass is so long I can barely see her, much less what she is after. A cottontail shoots out of the weeds, running across the tops of my boots!

"Rabbit coming at you!" I yell to Brian.

The only thing we see is the wake in the grass as the bunny zips along out of sight, both dogs thirty yards behind it. When Brian lifts his gun, shooting, John and I both laugh.

"Did you see it?" John asks him.

"No, but I saw where it was."

I tell him if he ever does that again, he better be good and sure where Maggie and Ted are.

"I checked, and saw them coming—don't worry. You're not gonna get them if you don't shoot, you know."

"Old 'grass shot' McCoy," we laugh.

The laughter ceases when Maggie emerges carrying the dead rabbit. Downplaying Brian's success, we tell him just how lucky he is. He insists on attributing it to skill. But ten minutes later, when Maggie flushes another rabbit and again all we can see is the blades of grass moving out ahead of her, Brian does exactly the same thing. This time, Ted fetches the rabbit to me. Brian asks us if we'd now like to rescind our insults about how lucky he was.

"No, we wouldn't," I tell him as I toss the unlucky rabbit to him, perhaps a little too hard.

Brian is all smiles as we cut south across the field toward a stand of young poplars. Lagging behind us, Maggie and Ted start feeling the heat. The stand of saplings juts out into the field at a narrow point. Brian and I enter the trees from opposite sides. Without warning, a woodcock flutters toward us. We both get our guns up, but before we can find the triggers, the bird drops between us, out of sight in the branches and leaves. There doesn't seem to be anywhere for it to hide but—although Brian and I are only a few yards apart—the bird is nowhere to be seen. The three of us watch intently as Maggie and Ted begin scouring the saplings. Wherever the woodcock is, I admire its nerve. When the dogs have crisscrossed the opening several times, I wonder if the little timberdoodle ran away. Finally picking up the scent, Maggie has her nose a foot from the bird and it still holds tight. Her nose touches it before it finally twitters up and out of the saplings. At the shot, the woodcock falls and is pounced on by both dogs. Maggie is getting the knack of how she has to react if she wants to make the retrieve.

She promptly rushes Ted and chases him back thirty yards with a series of vicious snarls and snapping teeth. He looks dazed, as if he has just barely escaped a mauling by a mountain lion. Maggie has no competition for the fetch as she happily carries the fat woodcock to the three of us. Just to be fair, I toss the woodcock into the puddle and let Ted, still keeping a cautious eye on Maggie, fetch it back to me.

Scouring the saplings, hedgerows, and fields, we hunt until almost dark. The sun, teetering just above the tree line, is a blood-red globe. The mosquitoes have returned and our T-shirts, not standard October hunting wear, are soaked with sweat. Although there's a good half-hour of hunting time remaining, the dogs are suffering in the heat. Panting a little too much, they're following on our heels instead of bouncing merrily along in front of us. They've run hard for two straight days now and will for the next few weeks. At home, for the duration of pheasant hunting season, they'll do nothing but sleep, looking like big, furry throw rugs. Moaning and groaning like old men, they'll manage to get themselves up only long enough to eat or drink. But, hitting the fields in the mornings, they'll be nothing but heart and fire, enthusiasm and spirit. Sprawled in the back of my truck, they're already sleeping. Patting their heads I close the hatch, leaving the windows open so they catch some of the cool breeze that just kicked up.

Sitting at the edge of the field, John reminisces about Mike and how he wishes he were here. Brian and I chide each other about his brush-shot rabbits. With the six-pack and the glass jar of jerky vanishing rapidly, we remember our pheasant hunts last year. Talking about the things we laughed at then, I wonder what we'll be laughing about this time next year. The sun, finally lost behind the far hedgerow, illuminates the underside of the sky in a warm glow, not unlike the fiery view through the darkened glass window of an old woodstove. With the conversation waning, the three of us just sit looking out over the field with its trees and grasses now bathed in the color of warm lava.

The day is winding down, and the season is heating up. Closing my eyes, I try to lock every moment of the day into memory. Some of them have already faded, but they'll come back. In time.

October 23—Epitome

Certain days afield take on a life of their own, becoming a benchmark, a reference point. These are the days to which other days during other seasons will be held up and compared. Months from now, locked in the cold depths of late winter, I'll think of these days when I think thoughts and dream dreams of the coming season. Sometimes the reason these days are so specially marked is success. Sometimes it's miserable failure—like swimming for the lost goose in the swamp. Little did I know when I rolled out of bed this morning, suffering the aches and pains of two hard days afield, today would be one of those days.

Brian and I work the fields, once again searching the same hedgerow and same patch of old vineyard posts for the same rooster that escaped on opening day. Once again though, the dogs come up empty-handed. The rooster is too smart to stick around with all the pressure we've been putting on it. Turning the dogs up the hedgerow running east from the road, we plunge deep into the heart of the huge fields. The pheasants we shot opening day came from the scrubby dogwood and grass of the field, but this time I send the dogs into the thick hedge, harshly telling them "get in there, get in there" every time they pop out of the row. Last year, Arnie and I came here. He had Katie, his pointer, and I had Maggie. The dogs chased a rooster, running invisibly along the ground, from the relative safety of a thick dogwood patch into the

Ted doing what he loves best.

dense cover of the thick hedgerow. That bird was a master of escape. Running the dogs from the road to the end of the hedgerow—two hundred yards more—it refused to flush. Arnie and I sprinted along each side of the row, desperately trying to keep up. Running hard, we managed to get to the end about twenty yards behind the dogs. Instead of flushing to our waiting guns, though, the bird turned and somehow weaseled between the dogs, running all the way back to the road. Easily outdistancing dogs and men, it had the speed of a roadrunner. Finally flushing back at the road, it was fifty yards ahead of the dogs, who were grunting and snapping branches, suffering the slings and arrows of the vicious hedgerow. Forty yards behind the dogs, Arnie and I watched helplessly as the huge bird soared over our trucks parked by the ditch. Taunting us with several hearty cackles, it quickly disappeared into the posted land across the road.

Releasing the dogs from the confines of the hedgerow, I give them a chance to open up and stretch their legs. Running separate scent trails, Maggie and Ted each get birdy. Ted angles back toward the road while Maggie bounds to the east. Brian and I don't have time to worry about who should chase which dog because, a moment later, the two birds take wing. Swinging the gun along after the closest one, I slide the safety off. The shotgun seems to bog down in midair, not moving fast enough. It's an easy shot, but as the barrels of the shotgun reach the bird's plump body, I recognize the mottled brown features of a hen pheasant. Quickly adjusting, I try to get the bird nearer to Brian aligned with my barrels.

"Hen!" Brian yells to me as I see him lowering his gun.

Heart pounding, I lower my own shotgun. Cracking twigs and bulldozing through brambles, the dogs have already resumed working. They don't want us to calm down after the two hens. Keeping us on our toes, they flush several robins and blue jays. The flutter of wings that they make is not unlike that of a woodcock, so when a woodcock blasts out of the thorny mess with Maggie hot on its tail feathers, it is excusable that Brian and I miss it. Flying north to another hedgerow, the bird lands in the exact spot where I shot my first woodcock over John's Mike.

When we finally break out of the front field and into the greater expanse of the huge old vineyard beyond, a rabbit skitters across the opening to my right as another disappears into a pile of old posts. Jumping on the pile, with Brian and the dogs watching, I try to spook it out. Holding her right front paw up and staring down at the base of the pile where the bunny disappeared, Maggie holds a classic point. A bunny point. But the rabbit holds its ground, and who can blame it?

A hen gives us a good run down the length of one of the rutty old grape patches, and when it finally flushes out the end, I'm so certain it's going to be a rooster I nearly convince myself it is one. Shaking my head, I try to clear my eyes, pulling my finger free of the trigger guard. Maggie, apparently frustrated by our lack of shooting, bounds across the field after the slow-flying hen and needs three harsh blasts on the whistle to convince her to return. As if to remind me of her worth, Maggie promptly picks up scent again. This time Ted is slightly out ahead of her and cuts off the bird, which again runs a surprising distance with both dogs in hot pursuit.

"This has got to be a rooster," Brian says.

Again, in a great flurry of wing beats, a hen lifts to the sky. Brian and I both pick up our guns, pretending to shoot it. This time it's Ted racing off after the bird.

"Ted!"

Before he gets far, I hit the whistle, laughing as he stops and pees on a post, as if that's all he had intended doing. Glancing out of the corner of his eye to see if I'm really mad, he begins professionally working the field, acting as if I'd never called him. He's still goofy and young, but is he ever smart. The dogs are working well and I want to keep them enthusiastic, yelling at them only for major violations. I don't know how many birds they've put up today, but it's enough to earn a little leniency.

Trudging out into the sea of grass in the center of the block, we're anxious to be free of the old posts and their treacherous wire. This area, too, is severely rutted, but the wires and posts are mostly gone. Maggie, not stopping to check some nearby brushpiles, runs hard and straight with her nose up into the northerly breeze. Hearing the excited jingling of the metal tags on her collar, Ted quickly races up behind her. Trotting along with the dogs, I feel my hips are already stiff, aching with the jarring as we cross the deep ruts. This time, the animal shows no sign of flushing and I wonder if we are on a bunny. If we are, there's a chance I can call the dogs back. I blow the whistle, but it falls on deaf ears.

They are chasing a pheasant. The chase goes on, circling, doubling, through water, across the piles of posts, through two hedgerows, and finally halfway around a large pond, covering nearly two hundred yards. I'm beginning to think we may be on that elusive runner from opening day, but my heart sags as yet another hen takes wing.

With the dogs satisfying their thirst in the clear water of the pond, I nearly step on a rabbit. Not at all confident of the snap shot, I manage to hit it as it zips away through the green grass at the edge of the water. Brian chides me that it isn't really sporting to shoot at them until they're completely hidden in the grass.

"You got lucky yesterday, pal."

"Nope. Once would've been lucky. Twice has to be skill."

"*Hrrmph.*"

Making one more pass across the back of the block, we call it a day. The dogs, though still enthusiastic, are moving slowly. As the temperature again pushes seventy, the mosquitoes are getting bad again. Rather than work the remaining three hundred yards across the back, I signal the dogs toward the truck. Milling around between two big piles of splintery old grape posts, they're probably just stalling or sniffing old rabbit scent. I walk up behind them, telling them, "Go on, find the birds!" Responding dutifully, if not excitedly, they trot ahead of us. Cresting a slight knoll, we find the grass here shorter than anywhere else we've been. The ruts are more weathered, more manageable, but there is little ringneck cover.

I honestly don't know where the big rooster comes from. I don't see the dogs get birdy. I don't see it sitting in the sparse grass. Nevertheless, a huge ringneck is suddenly rising quickly. The only sound is the leathery flapping of its big wings. Right between Brian and me, it seems to hover, long tail feathers drooping heavily below it. The moment is frozen. A split second later the bird is in full flight, speeding for the little ditch and the thick hedge on the other side. Our guns roar and the big bird crumples but is carried in a long, graceful arc. Instead of immediately marking where the rooster went down, I foolishly look back for the dogs that are now racing in our direction. I send them in for the retrieve and they can't find the bird. The whole thing seems ridiculous and would probably be funny if we weren't facing the possibility of losing the day's only pheasant. We are in six-inch-long golden grass cover, looking for a huge, brightly colored bird that's obviously dead. We have two dogs, at least one of which can smell a field mouse at fifty yards, and we can't find the bird. Is it possible it hit the ground running? No, the feathers littering the ground tell us that it took a direct hit, if not two. Ted and Maggie vacuum the ground fruitlessly.

"Fetch," I tell them repeatedly. Circling me a few times, Ted looks sheepishly out of the corner of his eye as if to make sure I'm serious, then bounds to Maggie's side to see if she's on anything. Brian spots something. Bending over and picking up the giant pheasant, he has an evil gleam in his eye.

"That's OK, I'll do your dogs' work for them," he says sarcastically, holding the bird up. He's immediately mobbed by the dogs, who want to sniff and lick at the fallen ringneck. He holds it down for them.

"At least we got it," I tell him, relieved.

"We? Oh sure. Now we got him."

"OK, wise guy, do you think you are the only guy I could have taken hunting today?" I ask him.

"Yep," he says, smiling.

The River

The morning's sun and blue sky are washed away by afternoon rain. There's only about two hours of daylight left, and easily fifteen minutes of walking, so we hurry down to the path. The water is unusually high. The little creek is muddy, coursing through places on the bank where we'd normally walk. If the river is this high, there won't be anywhere to stand and hunt.

Halfway to the river, under steadily darkening skies, John suddenly raises his hand and slips the shotgun off his shoulder. Turning halfway around, he holds up two fingers and whispers, "Stay down, and get ready."

Unsnapping the leash from the D-ring, I slip my hand firmly under Ted's collar. He lunges at the sound of the leash being unhooked but sits calmly back when he realizes he's still restrained. Taking a few steps, John holds his shotgun straight out in front of him. I am a few yards farther back from the bank and wish I could see more. There's a large oak tree lying at an angle from the bank with its top in the water. John moves haltingly toward it. From the peace sign he flashes me, I'm guessing there are at least two ducks nestled in the thick snarl of branches. His careful stalk works, and he's only twenty yards away as the mallards—two hens and a drake—lift noisily out of the branches. His Browning roars twice, and the drake splashes into the muddy creek.

Letting Ted go, I tell him, "Fetch it up!" Already several yards downstream, the mallard is spirited away by the unusually strong current. Ted runs down the path for a short distance before leaping into the muddy creek. Swimming out to the duck, he lunges for its head, which in turn picks up and snaps its bright bill at him, landing a good bite on his snout. Making no other attempt, he turns, swimming hurriedly back to me. John peppers the bird with a single shot from his reloaded gun, and I motion Ted back out again. I'm not happy with how he hesitates.

"Fetch it up, now!"

His big, sad eyes look up at me from the muddy water, searching for confirmation.

"Back!"

Swimming slowly out to the duck, this time he grabs it, lets it go, then grabs it again, taking no more chances with the snippy drake. I breathe a sigh of relief when he finally grabs the bird by its bright green head and swims steadily toward John with it.

Whew!

Petting and praising Ted, John tosses me the mallard to put in the decoy bag. I resaddle myself with all the gear as John starts toward the river. The normally dry land is now under water. Though I can't see him, I hear John fall in front of me. The walk is absolutely treacherous. Even Ted stumbles and falls over the lumpy ground, its features hidden by a foot of murky water. A moment later I lose my balance, tripping on a hidden branch and falling flat on my face. My gun is under me, unloaded but completely submerged. The decoy bag, both straps firmly around my chest and shoulders, comes down on top of me like a ton of bricks. On the way down, I get a mouthful of smelly river water and mud. Icy water floods the top of my waders. Struggling to get back on my feet, I swear a blue streak as the decoy bag puts up a valiant effort to keep me down. Finally wiggling free of the chest straps, I right myself. Then the water drains from the top of my waders down into both legs, soaking the rest of me. I swear again, more loudly this time. Reaching John, I find that he's in worse shape than I am. He's soaked, too. He made the trek without the benefit of waders and is soaked right up to his waist.

"Did you fall, too?" he asks.

"Uh, yeah."

"I thought I heard a woman scream."

"That would be me."

John setting decoys in the chill of early morning.

There's nowhere to stand. The cattails are completely submerged. John rigs the decoys on what passes for "shore" while I drag them into the heavy, yet fairly slow current of the Niagara River. I can't set them out as far as we normally do. Although this place is on the bend of the main river, protected from its heavier currents, the water is too high. There's an outer sandbar twenty-five yards from shore. The wade out to it is usually only about waist deep. This afternoon I'm in to the top of my waders before I even get halfway. Coming back in a few yards, I set the decoys. Wading to shore, I get more as John rigs them up. After putting the last of the dozen mallard decoys out, I turn around to get the three goldeneyes John wants set at the outer edge of the spread. He isn't there. When I finally spot him downriver about fifty yards, he's waist deep in the water and chasing two of the mallard decoys that broke free from their anchor lines. He manages to snatch them up just as it seems they're going to get away. Dragging the two deeks behind him, he exits the water about seventy yards from me. Even at this distance, I can see the water dripping off his jeans.

"What the hell," he says as he appears in the brush behind me, smiling and holding the two escapees. "I was already wet." Now he's soaked. His jeans and the bottom half of his coat are dripping. His knee boots have to be emptied. Standing on one foot at a time, he pours them out.

"You want to quit?" I ask him.

"No, this is the kind of weather when they really fly."

The wind is kicking up out of the north, and the rain is coming down lightly but steadily. He's right, but an hour later all we've seen, other than a handful of diver ducks out in the middle of the river, is one flock of mallards who were coming right at us but flared out around our decoys. Dark will be here soon, and the wind has just shifted again, blowing right into our faces. It's terrible wind for duck hunting. Ted, shivering in the water next to me, is bored.

I get an idea. Taking the mallard drake out of the decoy bag, I give it to John and tell him my idea. He sloshes down the bank and out of sight. Ted, doing his best to sit calmly even though there is nowhere to sit, watches intently as I raise my shotgun. When I pull the trigger the dead drake flies, splashing into the water. Ted looks at me, hesitating.

"Fetch!" I yell.

Diving into the water, he swims hard in the strong current. This is his first river retrieve—however contrived it might be. Grabbing the duck firmly, he realizes that the faster current isn't going to give him time to check to make sure it's dead. He doesn't hesitate as he turns back to shore with the duck.

Good.

He drops it at my feet, where it floats stiffly in the cold water. After casually walking the bank to John, I hand him the duck to repeat the performance. After several repetitions, Ted doesn't hesitate a bit, getting the knack of swimming slightly downstream of the drifting duck to intercept it. Even if this is a lousy night of hunting and our shooting scares off any ducks that might be around, the practice is great for him. He proves to be a powerful, tireless swimmer, even after a dozen retrieves.

Stopping at the Burger King drive-up window, I buy Ted and me some hamburgers. Unwrapping one, I turn around to hand it to him, but he's already asleep on my waders in the back seat. I wave the burger under his nose and he wakes up just long enough to wolf it down in a single gulp before his eyelids sag and he falls asleep again, eyes squinted, shivering.

At home he curls up with Maggie on the rug next to my bed, still a trace of a shiver racking his body. Greta says Mag hasn't budged since I brought her back from pheasant hunting. Maggie, who normally doesn't welcome Ted's company, at least in this proximity, has her eyes tightly shut and doesn't move as he rests his broad black head across her back.

"Good dogs. Good dogs."

October 24—A Strange Day, Indeed

Setting decoys in the river in the predawn hours is a surreal and not altogether unpleasant activity, if you can stand the cold. Upriver, the lights from Buffalo cast a warm glow on the chilly water. Across from us, streetlights and stoplights, cars and trucks, are visible in the Canadian suburbs of Niagara Falls. There is so much artificial light on the water that the penlights we use to set the decoys are almost unnecessary, except when messing with the inevitable knots and tangles in the decoy cords. Tom and I silently rig the decoys, followed along in the water by Ted and Jake. The dogs usually wait on the bank while we do the setup, but today they seem strangely anxious to be in the water. As long as they stay out of the decoy lines, their presence isn't unwelcome.

Legal shooting starts at one half-hour before sunrise. At one half-hour before sunrise, we're ready. The guns are loaded. Gear is stowed behind trees, camo netting strewn between bushes. Ted is curled up at my feet and Jake is sitting bolt upright at Tom's side, staring out over the river. Motioning for Ted to look at Jake, I want him to see how a "real" duck dog is supposed to act.

Ted is already snoring.

The flights begin a few minutes before sunrise. There aren't many—perhaps four or five separate flocks—but the number of ducks in each flock is absolutely staggering. Two or three big rafts of bluebills pass a half-mile out over the open river. In each flock are several hundred birds. We stay low, ducking our heads behind the blind. It's flocks like this that occasionally have a dozen or so break off from the main group to check out a spread of deeks. Our spread is not huge by Niagara River standards, but it should be adequate. We have a dozen mallards, two dozen bluebills, a dozen or so goldeneyes and a handful of canvasbacks. Our spread looks impressive, if not to the ducks, at least to Tom and me. But the wind is wrong.

For the next hour, a few ducks break off from the larger flocks, but after giving us a long-range once-over, they decide not to break tradition and land with the tailwind, which now drives fine, cold mist into our faces. The wind is now strong enough that we can see the water pick up off the whitecaps before it blows into our numb, red faces. Both dogs are now curled up like puppies at our feet. Even the mighty Jake has given up watching for ducks. Getting up to stretch my legs, I walk down to the boat launch. It's a sure bet that if I leave the blind, Tom will see some ducks. It never fails. You sit all day and see nothing, but once you get up and mill around—stop paying attention—the ducks fly in.

Braving the wind, two fishermen in yellow rain ponchos stand on the end of a long wooden mooring slip. One of them pulls in a big yellow perch as I watch. When Ted starts galloping in the direction of the launch—having just chased two seagulls out of the parking lot—I whistle him back. One of the fishermen walks to the end of the dock, leaning over to give Ted a pat on his big, blocky head, which he eagerly accepts, despite my whistle. He then turns back to me, as if he has just heard the whistle.

Back at the blind, I'm surprised Tom hasn't seen any ducks. He's been patiently waiting for me to get back so he could go relieve himself. Despite the conditions, he didn't want to leave the blind unattended. "They always come in when no one's watching," he says, mirroring my thoughts.

Tom disappears into the big trees on the bank, downriver from the blind. A moment later, a groggy-eyed Jake stands and trots down the bank after Tom. Five minutes later Tom stumbles out of the trees, shaking his head, holding his soaked hunting coat in front of him. The chest straps of his waders are hanging at his sides. The look on his face is not a happy one.

"Can you please pick up the decoys, Joel? I gotta get to the truck and see if I have any dry clothes."

"Sure," I say, stifling a giggle. I have a feeling I know what happened, but don't dare ask at this particular moment. Later on he'll tell me how he had just picked a nice slippery rock to stand on to take a leak. He had just gotten his waders and his pants down when—*wham* Jake knocked him face first into the mighty Niagara with his waders around his knees.

Back at the truck, he's found some dry clothes, but is still shaking from the cold. He's not a happy hunter. Jake, on the other hand, is sitting in the passenger side of Tom's truck and, through the fogged-up window, flashes me a big doggy grin, clearly pleased.

"I don't suppose I could swear you to secrecy about this," Tom says, eyeing me suspiciously.

"You could try."

More Adventures in Suburbia

Yesterday a calm morning led to a wild afternoon. Today, a torrential morning of duck hunting melts quietly into a sunny, pleasant afternoon. It's the first day of pheasant hunting that feels like an afternoon of bird hunting should. It's warm, nearly sixty degrees, but thanks to the twenty-four hours of rain, the sky has been sapped of its humidity. The long grass is wet, and that's enough to keep us cool, if not downright cold.

Tony, Brian, and I met at eleven and have been working the field hard ever since. I am dragging my tail pretty badly after getting up at four to duck hunt, and the pheasants are keeping me awake. We've already put up seven hens, driving the dogs absolutely mad, and it's only noon. At a quarter past twelve, the dogs pick up the scent of a rooster who runs down the field and part way into the next one before flushing wild, disappearing into a tiny hedgerow. The row is narrow—not fit to hide a chickadee, much less a rooster. Fanning out, the three of us follow as the dogs work the skimpy row, bordered by a mowed grass field on both sides. Even though the dogs race back and forth crazily—having seen the bird fly in here—they don't pick up the scent again.

We try everything. We beat brushpiles. We hunt the rows ringing the cut fields on all sides. We put the dogs down through the ditches.

Nothing.

Could it be that the bird swooped into the hedge—a feint— then simply passed through it, gliding on to some unknown patch of cover? They can't be that smart, can they?

At twelve-thirty, Brian has to leave. Actually he had to leave at twelve, but then we got on the rooster. Priorities, you know.

Tony and I follow the dogs through the patch of old grapevines where I flushed two hens with Brian the other day. It isn't long before two hens flush in front of us, flying directly to the little dry pond.

The early morning is catching up with me and I'm ready for a nap. Following the one remaining hedgerow to the road, I tell Tony about all the birds we've chased up and down this particular strip of cover over the last few years. With Maggie in the hedgerow to our left, I let Ted work the more open dogwood field to our right. I figure he's been up as long as I have, and, while I only had to wade in the river, he was out there swimming in it.

Along with Tom, of course.

Getting birdy for only a second, Ted flushes another hen on the way out. Nearly at the road, we're not too far from a new house that went up here a few years ago.

Tony points out the round patch of eight-foot high weeds near the roadside. "That looks like ideal cover," he says.

When I tell him that we've shot at least four roosters and three or four rabbits out of that tiny patch in the past few years, he looks at me skeptically.

I can't resist sending Maggie in, knowing she'll put out something. Rushing in, she's followed closely by Ted. The two of them disappear, engulfed by the little clump that's no more than twenty-five feet wide and perhaps twice as long. Tony takes a position at the north end. I take up a spot at the south side, holding my gun at the ready. Tony looks amused.

When Maggie blows out of the cover at my feet, huffing and snorting, I nearly fall over her. Making a mad dash for the hedgerow, she passes ten feet from me, but I can't even catch a glimpse of what she's after. Following her to the hedgerow, I hope I don't have to run to the other end, as we've done so many times in the past. But I don't have to worry about running. Once Maggie gets the rooster pinned in the cover, it flushes straight up. I don't raise the gun, though. The bird is directly between the house and me. Hovering for a moment, it can't decide which way to fly, finally opting for the open field. As it clears the house, swinging back toward the field, I hastily pull the gun up. Sliding the safe button forward, I let the shot go. If I had had time to think about it, I probably wouldn't have shot. The distance is at the far end of my shooting capabilities, and the severe angle and the high speed of the departing bird should call for some calculation of appropriate lead. I have no time to think about such intricacies.

Naturally, the bird falls from the sky as I consider kissing my new shotgun.

"Good shot!" Tony yells from behind me.

If you're going to bird hunt with somebody for the first time, it's always nice to have it be the day you make your once-in-a-lifetime shot.

The dogs disappear into the hedgerow. When they've been gone too long, I crash into the row myself and pop out onto the nicely landscaped lawn on the other side. The sight that greets me makes my heart rise into my throat. Maggie and Ted are racing along the lawnmower shed of the huge house. Ahead of them, the ringneck is speeding toward the birdbath.

Oh, boy. . . .

Twice, Maggie gets a grip on the bird's long tail feathers, and it whirls and pecks at her, beating its wings. The whole scene lasts only fifteen seconds, but it's a lifetime for me. Looking toward the house, I'm committed now. I race out across the lawn, praying the home owners are at work, just as Ted rushes in, knocking Maggie aside to pounce on the pheasant. Pinning it to the ground with his big paws, he holds his head up away from the snapping beak. Grabbing the bird out from under him, I begin jogging, herding the dogs for the shelter of the hedgerow. The rooster gives my forearms a good wing beating before succumbing. I'm still caught in the thorny hedgerow when Tony shoots. I'm totally unprepared for the sound, and the repercussion seems to explode in my head. The dogs, which have been behind me, letting me break the brush, suddenly sprint past me into the dogwood field. Shaking free from the hedge, I grab the branch of a thorn apple tree. I manage to somehow miss getting a palm full of thorns, but as one of the branches snaps up toward my face, an inch-long spike buries itself in the back of my left hand.

Ouch.

Tony is still standing there with his shotgun up when I exit the field. "Rooster," he says, still surveying the field. "Missed."

He'd been just standing there waiting for me when suddenly a ringneck flushed right up in front of him. Could it be that the second bird watched me exit the field and waited till it thought I was safely away before leaving the area? No, they're just birds. They're not demons. They simply cannot be that smart.

Can they?

October 27—The Runner

"Eeek eeek eeeeeeeek!"

My heart skips a beat as I jerkily bring the side-by-side up. But then I see Ted picking himself up, shaking off the effects of his collision. It's the third time he's run into one of the old wires strung around the vineyard. The noise is much like that of a flushing woodcock or—if the wind is right—a rooster pheasant. Looking questioningly at me, Brian wonders why I've shouldered the gun. Upwind from me, he hasn't heard the counterfeit flush. Zipping around twenty yards in front of him, Maggie is intent on nothing, investigating everything. She easily navigates the furrows and the old wire tangles, effortlessly ducking the wires as she weaves in and around the thornbushes.

I love watching my dogs work.

Maggie methodically scours the field, doubling and quartering, checking and rechecking. Ted dashes around in what seems to be haphazard fashion but, every now and then, surprises us by locking onto a scent. It's surprising that after a morning of walking we haven't flushed a bird. Not a hen. Not a timberdoodle. Nothing. I'd even like to see a rabbit. Maggie is so good on the cottontails I swear she's part beagle. Today not even a bunny cuts loose in front of us. Slow morning. I ask Brian where he thinks we should go, and he shrugs noncommittally.

We hunt our way toward a big irrigation pond, for lack of a better landmark. The pond is round and featureless, like all the other

New York limit—a rare occurrence for me.

watering holes dug out of this flat landscape. Its only saving grace is the lone mallard drake lifting silently from the water as we approach. Just for fun, I pick the gun up, pointing at the sky, watching Ted out of the corner of my eye. He snaps to attention, watching the duck's retreat.

"Where's Maggie?" Brian suddenly asks, not looking at me but searching the long grass.

"Uh oh," I say, looking for that familiar blur of brown and white.

"I'll bet she's on one," he says.

He's right.

When Maggie finally appears, she's all shoulders and nose. Zipping back and forth, she questions and verifies, snorting and sorting out scent.

"She's birdy," Brian says loudly.

We're fascinated as Maggie unravels the scent trail. Finally, after a dozen about-faces, she's off on a beeline.

"Runner!" I shout, now running myself. Brian is running, too.

As much as I hate these runners, I love them, too. For me they're the ultimate in pheasant hunting. Follow too close to the dogs, and the bird will run forever, never flushing. Let dog and bird get out too far ahead of you, and the bird will flush wild, out of range. At least you know there's a bird nearby. I'm sure there must be some bird-hunting rule against that, but there is no stopping Maggie.

I wouldn't want to.

Crossing a patch of open grass, she's snorting and sniffing wildly. Right on her heels, Ted, too, smells the intoxicating scent, matching her maniacal course turn for turn. I can't believe we didn't see the bird crossing in the clearing. Suddenly Maggie is headed back toward me, nose to the ground. I stop, waiting for the flush. As she makes a quick trip around a brushpile for a moment, I wonder if she might be on a rabbit. She's too excited for it to be only a bunny, though. Looking frustrated for a second, she's off again.

"This one's got to be good," Brian says breathlessly, coming up behind me.

Forty yards ahead of us, the dogs concentrate their efforts on a small dogwood patch. Suddenly, Maggie insanely bounces from right to left, then left to right. It must be right under her feet. At times like this I wish I could see what she's seeing down there in the grass. Can she see its tail feathers dragging the ground in front of her? Can she hear the sound of the bird's legs as they drag through the brittle grass? What's going on down there, Maggie?

I barely get the Stoeger up as the huge rooster takes flight. My legs are quivering from the run and my lungs and heart feel ready to burst. The bird's cackle is an insult, a goad. I pull the first and then the second trigger too fast, before the bird even completes its taunt. I see no feathers, no deviation of flight pattern, as it soars straight away across one field and then another. I sink to my knees, exhausted. Ted pounces on me and Maggie swings by, putting her paws on my chest to give me a quick kiss, forgiving me for the miss. When she takes off again, Ted stays by my side, his droopy bloodshot eyes looking at me quizzically.

"Did you see that bird, Teddie?"

His tail wags as he looks off to the side, thinking.

Brian again comes up behind me. "I saw where he went down," he says urgently.

"Then go ahead and get him," I say, whipped.

"C'mon, he's in the saplings. See that big golden tree hanging out over the field?"

"Yeah."

"He went down right in there."

"He hit the ground running, probably."

"No, he's got to be tired. Let's get him."

Trying to make the dogs heel to conserve energy is useless. Sensing the excitement in our voices and in our pace, they just can't stand staying at my side. Maggie, straining under the heel command, ready to run, looks longingly at me over her shoulder.

I give in, "OK, Mag, go on."

She scampers off to my right, not working too far out as we get closer to the rooster's landing area. She's engrossed in a blackberry bush when suddenly, and not surprisingly, a hen pheasant takes air, eventually circling around behind us. Brian and I both draw an imaginary bead on the bird as Maggie leaps after it, nearly catching it with one high vault. Turning back down the field, Ted starts after the hen. Snagging him on the way by, I turn him in the right direction. Five minutes later, we are in the area of the vineyard that must have been abandoned first when the grape operation shut down. The vines and posts here are in a worse state of disrepair than the rest of the field. They're nothing more than tatters of wood and coils and piles of rusty wire. Twenty-foot-high poplar saplings provide the shade that keeps the weeds down and makes perfect foraging cover for woodcock. We were in here just a few weeks ago with Arnie and his pointer. Katie pointed several woodcock and each time was promptly mugged by Maggie and Ted. In each case, the woodcock flushed wildly to the sky, much to the delight of my dogs. Arnie was getting exasperated, and he gently reminded me about training my dogs to "honor a point." Another rule, I suppose. There are too many rules to bird hunting.

The only solid clues to this field's agricultural past are the deep ruts gouged out between the wires. It's OK if a running bird goes straight out in front of you because you can run down the ruts. But heaven help you if one crosses the vineyard (they always seem to), because you're forced to run across the deep gashes, up and down, and just when you catch up to the dogs, you trip on a wire or fall into the brambles. You should see my brush pants.

Halfway down the second field, we're panting more heavily than the dogs when Brian motions in the direction of the big poplar, a globe of golden leaves decorating its top.

"This is where he went in," he says, stopping and watching Maggie intently.

Ten yards to my left, she's getting birdier by the minute. Ted, to the right, is also acting birdy. Suddenly, the rooster is in the air in front of Brian, cackling insanely as it picks its way deftly through the poplars at breakneck speed. Hoisting our guns, Brian and I each let two shots go through the saplings. Wounded branches rain down all around us. On the horizon the unscathed pheasant locks its wings, coasting back to earth.

"What the hell?" Brian asks.

"I saw where he went down," I offer.

"Yeah, me too. Back by the trucks, right?"

Although we've already covered a mile after this rooster, it would be foolish not to pursue it further, considering we have to go back to the road anyway. Another hen races out of the cover, flushing close in front of us, the dogs hot on its tail feathers. Again, we can't shoot.

The dogs, clearly disappointed with us, won't even look at me. The distance Brian and I chased this bird, only to miss it, is just a fraction of the ground Maggie and Ted have covered. Breaking through a thorn-laden hedgerow into the first field we hunted today, I spot our trucks out by the road. Maggie is sitting in the field waiting for us.

Sitting!

Working the field for the last time today, Ted is still happy (he always is), but little Maggie's demeanor is nothing like the animal I set free from the truck this morning. She trots dutifully around the dogwood bushes, but her bounce is gone. As she carefully sniffs a cattail-choked low spot in the field—where we killed this year's first rooster—it's clear that her enthusiasm is waning. My own enthusiasm is there, but my feet are wet, the ruts have played hell with my back and legs, and the missed shots still ring loudly in my ears, the way a good shot never does.

Suddenly, Maggie's nose is up into the wind. She stiffens, staring into the hedgerow.

Maggie guarding her ringneck from Ted, whom she chased off just before the photo.

    "Is that where he landed?" I ask Brian, whose eyes are fixed on Maggie.

Behind Maggie's own eyes, wheels are turning. Even Ted is staring at Maggie, respectful of her opinion and waiting for her cue. Crouching like a cougar, Maggie creeps up to the hedgerow, hesitating only briefly before suddenly pouncing into it. She is only in the wicked tangle for a moment when the rooster comes up. This time it doesn't tempt us with a cackle, knowing it's been had.

The bird is all business as its wings beat furiously to carry it out of gun range. I glimpse Ted running along under the bird that is rapidly gaining altitude. Two convergences happen in a blink of the eye. First, both my double and Brian's autoloader blast their loads of birdshot into the sky, catching the big ringneck in the crossfire. Second, both dogs converge on the fallen bird. I swear I hear their skulls crack as they rush in for the retrieve. Scrappy growls arise from the dogwood tangle just a moment before Ted emerges with the bird. Walking along with him, Maggie sniffs suspiciously to make sure it's really dead this time. Ted delivers the bird perfectly to my feet, where Maggie promptly snatches it up and puts it in my hand. I'm sure there's a rule about making your bird dog honor your Lab's retrieves. . . .

But who needs rules?

October 28—The Arrival

Haunting notes begin.
A song that smells
Of spruce and rock
Music that winds sinuously
Around us like smoke
Carried on a breath of wind

—Victoria Vest, from *Nakai's Flute*

It's a good, windy afternoon to hunt ducks. It's turning colder and the sun that occasionally poked through the gray sky this morning is now more deeply buried, hiding in the threatening clouds. Its warmth is now forbidden, its light nearly forgotten. The brittle gray-and-white trees in the swamp are shaken harshly, bullied by the wind, being forewarned that summer's kindness is gone and winter's harsh fury is not far away.

The decoys are set and the wind challenges me to get the canoe to shore. I'm relieved when the nose of the boat finally pushes into the weeds. Ted is restless, running up and down the bank, young and impatient. Dad is quietly working on the blind, stringing it between blowing bushes.

An hour later as we hide in the long grass, two gallinules—little half-duck, half-shorebirds—swim to the decoys, strutting through the water, not swimming at all like normal ducks. They dart dramatically left to right, right to left, and it's amazing they make any progress at all. Their bright orange beaks are comical beacons—clown noses—against their dull gray feathers. Having a pair of live decoys paddling around in the spread is good to draw in the other ducks, but where are all the ducks?

The warmth of Ted, asleep against my leg, permeates my waders. His light snoring is nearly lost in the breeze, his legs twitching as he dreams. Perhaps in his dreams, at least, there are ducks. Dad and John talk quietly, and over the soft lull of their voices, I hear something. Ted stirs in his sleep, his front paws reaching out toward the swamp in a long stretch. Does he hear it, too?

Aside from the two strange little gallinules, funny little refugees from a forgotten prehistoric era, the waterfowl are quiet. The birds we've seen for the past few weeks are mostly small resident family flocks of wood ducks, mallards, and geese. The big flocks, great waves of birds that will pepper the sky from horizon to horizon, haven't started coming in.

That is, until now.

Something makes me turn my back to the blind and face north. Five minutes before sunset, several huge flocks of Canada geese appear on the northern fringe of the waterfowl refuge. The geese, nothing more than black specks, have to be over a mile away. Could I have been hearing them a moment ago? No. They're too far out. But maybe. No longer wishing for ducks, or even thinking about them, I simply stare in awe at the sky as the living mass approaches us. The birds are silhouetted against the darkening sky, which, though it lacks the crimson hue of a classic waterfowl painting, has an intriguing and subtle grayish-pink tint. But a spectacular sunset isn't necessary because tonight it's the players that matter, not the stage dressing. Ted perks at the sound of their honking, which he hears long before I do.

The goose music is lonely and haunting and reverberates with images of wilder places than this. The music makers are

The first wave of the autumn goose migration.

coming closer. Instead of just a mass, I see the individual geese now, each with their white teardrop cheeks and long, fluid wing beats. Tensing at my side, Ted sits upright, watching the sky with his sad eyes. As I put my hand on his back, he leans his heavy body into me, watching the arrival. The first wave of geese, still flying high, passes over the highway, then suddenly drops, wings braking and bodies plummeting, like hundreds of living cannonballs, into the center of the refuge pool a thousand yards away. None of the birds breaks off from the flock and comes over into the hunting area.

Not a single one.

I wonder how the geese know to go to that very same spot year after year, particularly since migrating geese haven't been hunted here in years. When the geese are all down, a huge flock of mallards, whose arrival was hidden by the geese, begins circling the same section of the refuge. A few, breaking off the main group, turn slightly in our direction. Thoughts return briefly to hunting as seven mallards give us a flyover and we crouch behind the flimsy green blind. Trying hard not to look up and expose our pale faces to the passing birds, we're all eager to sneak a peek. In my peripheral vision, I see that I am not the only one looking at the sky. As the ducks—two drakes and five hens— bank away and head straight back for the refuge to join the other birds, John picks up his wooden call and makes a long, crying wail. The ducks pay him no mind, though, quickly dropping out of sight into the refuge.

The wind has died considerably since I set the deeks, and I'm thankful I won't have to paddle so hard to pick them up. As we stand on the dike, our watches tell us shooting time is over, though there is plenty of light left even on this overcast afternoon. Without the dike at our backs to block the sounds, the symphonic honking of the geese and quacking of the mallards in the refuge fill the air, which is now crisp and smelling of winter, with their excited cries of arrival.

The sound is of joyous return and renewal and makes me smile. The sound is of sadness and estrangement and makes me shiver, ducking farther into my coat for warmth.

The sound is pure autumn.

November

Cold mornings usher in colder days.
Autumn's grasp is firm.
The joyous warmth of summer,
Is forgotten in November's splendid wrath.

November 2—Long Walks

The dogs are restless and I can't keep them from running ahead, as our boots mire down in the muck of an old railroad bed. I've yelled. I've whistled. I give up. The dogs are going to the field without us.

"Maaaaaaaaaaaggie!" John finally yells, doing a fair impression of me.

Both dogs whirl, looking back at John. Perhaps it's the different voice. Either way, he gets their attention. Unhappily, they trot back. The long walk eventually rewards us with one flush, but when the pheasant bursts from the hedgerow, it flies directly into the sun before dropping out of sight on the other side of the hedgerow. Safety off, I'm blinded and don't pull the trigger. We comb the grainfield and the hedgerows. Crossing the field to the pond, we hunt around its fringes for bunnies. But we don't see another living thing.

The walk back somehow feels longer than the walk in.

Across the road, we endure another long walk to try a field I've never been to before. The cover is perfect, the fields gorgeous, and again we walk for hours and shoot nothing. We turn back toward the road, which is nowhere in sight, and the dogs jump two hens out of a hedgerow.

The walk back feels twice as long.

Finally, we head for the spot with the old vineyards—it's close to the road and we've shot several birds there already. Driving south, we pass out of the band of clear sky and sun that has been holding over the lake and into a gray squall. By the time we get to the field, there's an inch of snow on the hood of my truck.

Like overtired kids, the dogs aren't listening well and seem to have lost their enthusiasm. They aren't the only ones. Managing to flush two more hens, again we find no roosters. When we are halfway back to the open vineyards, two orange hats bob toward us, standing out like fireballs above the snow-covered brush. The guy and his wife are running a beagle for rabbits, and rather than spend an hour waiting for the three dogs to sniff one another's private parts, I swing wide around the other hunters, giving them a courteous wave. That will take us the long way out into the field. Once back there . . . well you can guess the rest.

No birds.

The walk back was murder.

November 3—The Untouchables

I wish I'd kept track of the number of birds we've seen. As another flight of two hundred canvasbacks passes from west to east over the water, I imagine the duck count would already be well into the thousands, and it's only ten o'clock. The day is perfect, with wind out of the west and light snow falling all morning. There is enough wave action to keep the birds stirred up, as well as enough to fill my chest waders when I was foolishly setting decoys in the pounding surf. The six bluebill decoys I managed to get out before the huge wave crashed over my head bob crazily in the muddy breakers. I'm already worried about having to retrieve them. They managed to draw in a goldeneye drake for a closer look, which Dad and I promptly missed, although we both emptied our guns.

Every other bird we've seen has been far out over the lake, where the waves aren't so violent. The flights of canvasbacks are followed by a large flock of geese, and though I'm sure they are honking, the sound is lost in the crashing of the waves on shore.

Nestled in a hollow against a high bank, our blind faces north to Canada. We are well protected from the harsh gusts. I don't understand why the wind is blowing from the west but the waves are coming from the north. Watching the weather forecast last night, I thought the west wind would cause the waves to come out of the west, ideal for this spot. But the waves crash right into us, squarely hitting the shore with their violent force. Sitting with his hands in his pockets, Dad is looking at the ground. Curled up against the muddy bank, Ted is sound asleep.

A time for conversation. Brian and Ken in a pheasant field.

What a miserable day, I think to myself, pouring another cup of hot coffee from my thermos.

Around eleven, the snow is falling heavily. Although I've already changed into dry clothes, my shivering is becoming more uncontrollable. During a short break in the howling of the wind, barely perceptible over the steady hiss and crash of the waves, we hear a strange noise. From nowhere, three whistling swans drop out of the clouds and fly over the blind. They're huge, beautiful. The sighting is so brief, and they disappear so quickly, it's as if they were never there. The image that burns in my mind is of three angels, teasing us with a glimpse of their white shimmering bodies and unearthly song. But they're gone now. All that remains are the waves and the cold.

Seeing my father and Ted huddled against the merciless weather, I grab my camera to snap some pictures. Climbing the high bank, I try to get a better angle on the blind, still getting the decoys and surf in the background. While raising the camera, I spot six ducks flying straight for the decoys. I drop the camera into the grass with a thump, pulling the shotgun off my shoulder. Trying to yell down to Dad, without being loud enough to scare the ducks off, I'm frustrated when he doesn't hear me.

"Here they come!" I finally yell, hoping that the ducks—I now see they're goldeneyes—won't hear. Dad snaps up, grabbing his gun as he searches the water. Crouching behind the blind, he spots the low flying ducks. Sensing the excitement, Ted races out of the blind and halfway up the bank. I'm out of the blind, in the open. Ted is out of the blind running toward me, and I have my doubts the little divers will finish their approach. I'm shocked when they flare two feet above the decoys, setting their wings to land. Picking out the closest drake, I shoot twice as it hovers above the bluebill decoys. Caught perfectly in the center of the shot pattern, it splashes down into the decoys.

Then it disappears.

My shotgun now has only one shell left in it, and all my extra ammo is in the blind. Of course.

"Dad, when he comes up, be ready to shoot!"

Dad has his gun pointed at the decoys, as do I. Moments pass. And we wait.

"Where is he?" Dad asks.

Suddenly the duck appears—not bobbing to the surface but rocketing out of the water, a feathered missile. I discharge my last shell in futility. Dad shoots, too, but the duck sails out into the open lake, apparently unhurt. Standing at the edge of the water, Ted waits for my signal to fetch. He never gets it.

The waves are hitting the beach more frequently, and a glance into the treetops behind us confirms the wind has again picked up. I decide it's now or never to go get the decoys. Even though my waders are still wet on the inside, soaking my dry shirt, I manage to dart in and out of the high, muddy waves in the right places and at the right intervals, pulling the decoys without incident. There are a few tense seconds during my final trip to shore as a huge wave—much bigger than the one that got me this morning—appears eighty yards behind me. Running the last few yards to shore—actually, in a slow-motion "moonwalk"—I get clear of the beach just as the wave smashes the shore, sending spray twenty feet into the air. Ted is now sitting on a boulder on the bank, and his face says, "Better you than me, pal."

Rounding a bend out in the dirt road, we spot a huge eight-point buck racing across a cut cornfield. It stops in the center of the field, appearing defiant as it stands looking at us. Not satisfied that we mean it no harm, it rushes back into the woodlot. As the buck bounds slowly back into the brush, its white tail flags us every ten yards or so, the deer's wide rack neatly missing the branches it runs through. It taunts us by stopping once more and looking back, somehow knowing that it is as untouchable as the rafts of ducks we can still see flying over the open lake.

In the back of the truck, Ted is already snoring.

November 5—Dad's Rooster

The place is tiny, merely a postage stamp. It's maybe two acres, bordered on one side by the main highway, enveloped on the other three by a monstrous cornfield. Trucks roar by on the road, hustling from Rochester to Buffalo with load after load of who knows what. I keep Maggie and Ted leashed until we're well into the field and away from the road. I'd hate to end the season by getting one of them run over.

When I let them loose, they work quickly through the sparse grass, eager to check out this new spot. The dogs, used to working thicker cover, move effortlessly through the field. I've been here before but only with John and his Mike, never with Ted and Maggie. Pointing to the southeast, John reminds me where Mike put up a nice rooster for us a few years ago. He's still thinking about his dog as I whistle for mine, using a flick of my hand to signal them to that spot. Dad stays on the field edge as the dogs work a little tangle of wild grapevines between the field and the corn. Cars on the main road slow to watch us, our bright orange not offering any concealment in the open field.

I'd like to get a rooster for Dad. I don't think he's been with us once this year when we've shot one. He always says he's my bad luck charm, and I feel bad about that. I hope the birds cooperate tonight. I'd like to see him get a shot.

With the sun hovering just above the western horizon, the little grass field and the huge sea of corn are bathed in red. I can imagine a rooster bursting to the sky, the sun's color reflecting off its brilliant plumage in that frozen moment before the hunters raise their guns. But the dogs run listlessly, focusing on no particular scent. I can already tell this little hastily devised postwork hunt is going to be another bust. It's near the end of the season and the roosters that haven't been shot—particularly in heavily hunted areas like this—are full of tricks and surprises.

Maggie, deep in the snowy brush, trying to flush just one more bird.

The entire hunt lasts less than twenty minutes, and, too quickly, we reach the end of the field. Stopping twenty yards shy of the corn, we stand in the setting sun, enjoying the cold air and the clear fall sky. Dad and John sling their guns onto their shoulders as I rest the stock of mine on my boot, wrapping my hand around the fat double barrels. Without gloves on, the metal feels numbingly cold. Shooting the breeze, we watch the dogs chase each other, playing tag in the long grass. Finally, with darkness approaching, we briefly discuss hunting the grass field once more but think better of it. The cover here is too sparse to hide a bird from three men and a dog, and going back over it is pointless. Even the dogs know this, or they'd already be at it. While we are talking, Maggie dashes toward the corn. Suddenly turning, she runs in front of my dad, head down. In a single bound, she disappears into the corn. Ted dashes in behind her, tail wagging furiously, nose to the ground. Once they are inside the cover of the corn, Maggie lets out an excited yelp.

She's on one.

"Great," I say to no one in particular, wondering how far the bird will run my dogs. The cornfield stretches nearly as far as the ridge. I wouldn't be surprised if the pheasant ran all the way to the end before flushing—if it ever does. We clearly hear the dogs crashing through the crisp stalks, their sound coming from the left, then the right, then the left again. Running circles, the bird evades rather than outdistances them. My heart pounds as the crashing nears. I hear it cackle, flushing. Wings flap, yet I see nothing. The rooster uses one of the rows of corn as a hidden runway to gain momentum. By the time it clears the tops of the stalks into our line of sight, it has attained flight speed. It is a golden blur, its tail feathers not drooping but blowing straight out behind it. An inch of white rings its neck. This is a huge bird.

The only one in position to shoot is my dad, and it's a long shot. With him angling rapidly away, hitting the bird will require a fair amount of luck. I'm not surprised Dad doesn't shoot, and I don't say anything as he lowers his gun.

"Should I have shot?" he asks.

John and I both hesitatingly agree that we would have tried.

"Well, how come you didn't shoot, then?" he asks me, sounding frustrated with himself.

"You were in the way."

"You should have told me to shoot!" he says.

He is silent, but I'm happy he saw a rooster. He finally got the chance to shoot, even if he blew it.

"Welcome to the club."

November 8—Return to Paradise

As we descend into the valley, the wind howls and the sky is slate gray, threatening to open up at any second. The trees—still sparsely dressed when we were here in October—are now stripped bare, their trunks exposed. The ground is covered with their discarded leaves. Any leaves bold enough to remain will be scoured away and sent earthward after today's wind. The hemlock tree stands as a silent sentinel in the orchard, its dark green majesty enhanced by the lack of leaves on the trees around it. The apples that still clung to the trees in occasional clusters last month are all on the ground, and there aren't many of those left. The deer have been stocking up for winter. Behind me, Dad carries the backpack full of straps and ropes and gadgets we need to hang the tree stand. The shoulder straps on the heavy stand dig into my shoulder, and I'm thankful our destination has finally been reached. Down in the orchard valley, the wind is nonexistent. The treetops, blowing in the gales on the hill above us, seem to be in another world.

The calm of the valley has always made it my favorite place to deer hunt. If I hadn't already been lucky enough to get a deer, I would be setting my stand here again. I've still got a doe permit to fill, but am more interested in getting Dad a deer, knowing this is the spot to do it.

Unfolding the sections of the ladder, I jam the first two pieces together with a metallic clink that resounds through this island of quiet in the sea of wind. On cue, a huge eight-point buck rises from a pile of brush forty yards from the stand, racing down into the creek bottom and quickly disappearing in the hemlocks. A split second later, a doe and fawn bolt from the same spot, following the buck's route downhill. Dad and I watch in stunned silence. The big buck—definitely the one I saw in October—was bedded only yards from the hemlock. When Dad asks if I'd rather hunt this stand again, I remind him I only have a doe permit left to fill. And I'd like to see him get a crack at the big buck. A few years ago he sat in the hemlock stand, deciding to climb down and take lunch early. Unbeknownst to him, a big buck—perhaps even this buck— had quietly come in and bedded down behind him. When Dad slung his leg off the stand onto the ladder, he was treated to the sight of the big buck rising to its feet just a few yards behind him.

He just has to be thinking about that.

John will be coming in tonight and once Dad's stand is set, we search for a spot to put up a stand for John. I decide on an area I've been meaning to bowhunt for years. It's a small patch of white pines above one of Doc's bigger ponds. It's where the grouse did the ground-dance on me, nicely evading a load of birdshot. There is a narrow break between the small stand of pines and a larger pine stand up the hill. The open area has two small apple trees and the ground around the trees is streaked with deer trails. There is a small notch in the pines, where we lean John's ladder stand against a tree. It fits perfectly. Clearing away some branches, I sit in the tree stand and envision a deer coming up the closest trail, only ten yards away. A berry bush, directly between the stand and the trail, looks as if it was placed there just for our purposes. When a deer steps behind it, John will have a chance to draw. It's the ideal setup. After a little more adjusting and tinkering, we leave the block of pines, scaring up two grouse as we go.

In the pasture the wind is howling and the rain is coming at our faces sideways. It is a miserable day. At least the rain will have a chance to wash our scent off the tree stands and out of the deer trails before we hunt. Hunting today is looking out of the question. There's always tomorrow.

"Who's bothering my deer?" a familiar voice booms out of the pines on the hill above us.

Howard, my father-in-law, comes down the hill. I can see by the look on his face that, despite the rain, he is caught in the intoxication of this magical place. He hasn't been here in months and looks the way I felt first setting foot back here in October. In town visiting Myrtle and Howard Sr., he has decided to come up and work on his deer stand for rifle season, now only a few short weeks away. Clearing shooting lanes and piling rocks, he's making sure everything is just right, so on opening day of deer season he can just walk in and shoot a deer. One-two-three. We laugh.

Walking to a place in the pasture that's overgrown with beech saplings and punctuated by gnarled oaks, he shows us an incredible runway. The trail wasn't here last year. The meadow grass is worn down to the bare dirt and the trail snakes in and out of the beeches. Every fifty or sixty yards, the bark of the saplings is rubbed bare. The rubs are all fresh. At the edge of the pasture lot, the trail intersects a larger trail. The larger trail runs down the narrow corridor between the beech saplings and a two-acre patch of thick, thirty-foot high spruce trees. I've never seen a more heavily used deer trail. Careful not to step in it, we search for a tree in which to hang my stand. Changing my mind, I climb ten trees before I find one I want. One tree is too close. One is too far. One is too tall. Another is far too short. One is perfect but just doesn't seem right. Howard and Dad wait patiently, occasionally shaking their heads. We are all soaked to the bone as the rain comes down even harder. I finally screw the tree steps into the trunk of a twisted, ancient beech, just twenty yards from the deer trail. Once the stand is hung, I sit to check the view. My dad removes a couple of branches between the trail and me. Gingerly stepping onto the trail, Howard holds his hands above his head like a funky ten-point rack and saunters down the trail. I laugh as he swings his rack from side to side.

"You're an easy shot," I tell him, drawing my bowstring.

"Good. Now let's get the hell out of here," he says, shaking the water off his hat.

Taking a last look up at my stand, I notice a big hole on the opposite side of the trunk. I point it out to Dad and Howard.

"If that's a squirrel hole, I'm going to be in trouble."

Quickly hushing me, they hurry me away from the tree before I can change my mind again.

Howard, Dad, and I have dinner with Myrtle and Howard Sr., hashing over old stories and new hopes, discussing Greta and the kids and the next time they can come with me. The usual. Howard Sr. says that, while we were up on the hill, there was a countywide tornado warning. I'm glad we decided to delay hunting until tomorrow.

After a slice of Myrtle's apple pie, Dad and I retire to our sleeping bags in the basement, turning in early after a long day traveling and scouting. Waking up once, I see that the little digital clock reads 2:00 A.M. and I vaguely wonder where John is? The thought is lost as I drift back down into darkness.

November 9—Saturday

The alarm clock sounds too early. I'm tempted to reset it and go back to sleep. Gradually, it dawns on me in the cool dark of the basement that the wind is no longer howling outside, and the rain is no longer pelting the windows. The fact that it may be a beautiful day to hunt gradually creeps into my foggy mind, finally slapping me awake. The excitement is back. Wiggling my way out of the sleeping bag, I stagger toward where the light cord is dangling unseen from the ceiling. Sweeping my arms out in front of me, I search for the cord, taking careful steps in the thick blackness. My foot connects solidly with something that shouldn't be there.

"Ouch!"

John. More specifically, John's head.

Over a fast breakfast, John tells us that Route 17 was flooded out by the river. He was rerouted through the hills and several times considered simply turning around and going home. At one point he ended up telling off a fireman who was waving people toward the detour, taking great glee in not telling John which way to go. His five-hour trip had turned into a nine-hour nightmare, and he looks like hell.

A half-hour later we are back on the hill, still hidden in darkness.

Dad disappears down over the knoll, the beam of his flashlight bouncing up on the trees from time to time as John and I hike toward the pond. Doc's house is quiet and dark. We're careful not to turn on our own flashlights until we are away from the house. I walk John to his stand, which he hasn't seen yet, handing him up his bow. I point at the berry bush, miming the action of drawing a bow. He smiles and nods.

I don't have any trouble finding my tree but am shocked at how I find it. The base of the tree is now in a brook. The little rivulet running through the center of the beech saplings has flooded its bank, engulfing a twenty-foot wide swath of the woods, including the base of my tree. After sloshing through the water, I quickly climb the slippery steps. Daylight is a long time coming. Although the rain stopped some time in the night, my pants are soaked from the walk in the long grass near John's stand. Long before the sun even thinks about coming up, shivers make paths up and down my back. A lone "yip" echoes down from the rocky ridge to my south. The sound, incredibly sad, is answered by a dozen more as the mountain's coyotes sing together one last time before sunrise.

Eyes closed, I remember the first time I hunted alone in the Adirondacks. I spent the day deep in the mountains bowhunting alone. Coming out of the woods, barely trusting my compass, I still had a quarter mile to go to the main road. All around me, coyotes started howling, and they were close. I found the road fast.

The wails echoing off the high ridges and below me in the valley send an elemental shudder through me. The urge to nod off is strong, but I don't want to wake up three hours into daylight to find ten deer standing around me. In the dark woods the lack of visual stimuli battles my consciousness. Cinching up my safety belt, I turn my head to the sky, looking at the dizzying array of stars layered up through the heavens. The moonless night gives away all its secrets, but even they aren't enough to keep me awake.

When I return from my dream (there were coyotes in it), the sky is still dark, but the stars are disappearing in a gauze of gray and dim yellow slowly creeping in from the east. The features of the surrounding woods gradually become clearer. The area has changed dramatically since yesterday afternoon. There is water everywhere and branches lie scattered around the woods, their freshly broken ends showing brightly against the drab landscape. A large, dead beech lies on its side—it was standing when we left yesterday. I wonder if a tornado did come through here.

The woods are calm. Last night's wind has died with the rain. Instead of the hushed silence of dawn, the sound of the newly formed brook fills my ears. This is going to be a problem. I like hearing the crunch of hooves in the leaves or the sound of a doe's low grunt as it talks to its fawn. I like hearing the squawking blue jays and the chattering squirrels. I like to hear the flutter of a chickadee's wings as it flits around my camouflaged face. Or the sound of a downy woodpecker as it tap-tap-taps on the trunk of my tree, searching for a meal. All I'll hear today is the babbling and bubbling of the wayward water trying to find its way back home.

The sun is up now and I could swear the water is even louder. Turning my head this way and that, moving more than I should, I try to catch a glimpse of deer slipping through the woods. Even if the beech leaves covering the ground weren't soaked and quiet— even if they were their usual crunchy selves—there's no way I could hear a deer coming. Hunting today is going to be strictly visual, so I continue craning my neck slowly, knowing I'm making too much movement but not knowing what else to do. I don't want to be surprised by deer appearing unexpectedly.

The sun has been up only an hour when I realize this spot is not going to work. By the look of the pool of rainwater on the knoll above me, feeding this mini-river, this stand is not going to be good all weekend. My confidence starts slipping. I want out, having no desire to waste the morning here. At the same time, I know I'm on a great trail, the conditions are good, and the sound of the brook will cover my sounds as well as those of the deer. I convince myself to stay until noon at least. I'm an outdoorsman. I'm up to a little adversity. I can take it.

Then the squirrel comes out.

A warning would have been nice—a little scratching of claws on bark, a little early morning chatter, or rustling leaves and branches. But no, there's no such warning. The squirrel makes its appearance suddenly, materializing six inches to the right of my face. It's just there.

This squirrel knows a man doesn't belong fourteen feet up a tree with his rear end parked next to its front door, but I have to give it credit—if not for its smarts, at least for its cool. Instead of letting go with a woods-alerting warning chatter and diving for its hole, the squirrel races around to the other side of the tree. I hear it on the bark, now six inches to the left of my head. I resist the urge to turn my head and look at it, since I know that would be the end of its coolness. I hear a soft "putt-putt-putt." In an instant, the animal rings the tree again, looking right into my camouflaged face. Its sides puff in and out as it once again talks softly to me. I try to stifle a chuckle as it inspects me. After hanging onto the smooth beech bark next to me for a moment, it scoots up the tree. Again, I resist the urge to look up, knowing it would spook the creature into a chattering fit.

I'm in a bad spot now. Scaring my new friend will ensure that it won't return to its hole until I've gone. What it will do is sit up in the top of some tree screaming at me, trying to convince me to do just that. But so far so good. I don't know where it is, but I know it's still above me. A few moments later, the squirrel appears on a narrow branch fifteen feet above me. It scurries out on the limb, balancing with its tail until it reaches a nearby sapling that still has several beech nuts in its top. Meticulously cutting a nut, the creature races back toward the tree, pausing briefly to peer over the branch at me before jumping onto the tree. It's as if it just wants me to know it knows I'm there. As long as the squirrel's quiet, that's fine with me. Over the course of the next half-hour, it keeps me entertained with its nonstop trips to the saplings, cutting one beechnut at a time, then rushing back to the tree with them as if they were hot to the touch. I'm actually disappointed when the trips end and the fat bushytail returns to its hole on the other side of the tree.

Around ten, the babbling water is beginning to give me a headache. My muscles are stiff from the cold and from remaining motionless. I know the sound of the flowing water will hide some of my noise, but it also makes it more difficult for me to know how loud my movements are. I lean back against the beech and close my eyes for a few minutes, trying to ward off the headache before it gets worse. I think of the upcoming rifle season, and how good it will feel to have the gang back together again. Thinking of past bow seasons and past deer, I hear the laughter of friends in the bubbling of the water as it subtly lulls me to another place. The headache retreats behind the memories.

A light gust of wind blows the snow into my face. The snow? There is no wind . . . no snow . . . I'm beginning to fall asleep. Memories fill my subconscious, enhanced by the real smells and sounds of the woods around me. I blink my eyes, trying to come out of it, but the trance is too deep and the memories are too tempting. I am soon dreaming.

The tiny flashlight beam bounces around the snowy woods, arcing off branches just as they slap me in the face. Every now and then the light catches a stray deer track, ghostly and promising in the dark.

I haven't hunted the birch stand in years and I'm not only hoping the tree is still standing, I'm not even sure I can find it. I decided after crawling into my sleeping bag last night that I'd come up here and search for the "three birch" stand. I had a bad experience there a few years ago and I haven't hunted it since. I'd arrowed a three-point buck that ran downhill with enough momentum to carry it onto the neighbor's property. They happen to be the neighbors that abhor hunting in general and really hate hunters specifically. The deer came to rest only a few feet from their woodshed. I couldn't believe that the heart-shot deer had gone so far so fast. Removing the deer from their property took some diplomatic maneuvering, to say the least.

As I finally crest the top of the hill, my back is soaked with sweat. My seven-pound bow has doubled its weight and the tree stand's straps dig into my shoulders at every step. Shining the flashlight around the woods, I try to get my bearings. To my right is the big cherry tree I was sitting against when I shot a six-point buck here a few years ago. I remember that day well because after I shot the deer, dressed it, tagged it, and hauled it down the mountain, I realized I had left my knife back up on top. After the long climb back up, I sifted through the gut pile, not able to locate the knife. Once I was immersed to my elbows, I spotted the knife nearby, neatly closed and placed on top of a rock, presumably so I wouldn't lose it. Reaching into my coat, I feel for the familiar shape of that old knife.

In a moment, I'm in the birch blowdowns and know I've gone too far. The small stand of birches I'm looking for is due south of here. I carefully pick my way over brittle tops and fallen trunks, long stripped of their whiteness. I remember turkey hunting in here and watching a bloated, pregnant doe staggering around miserably, bedding and getting up three times before gradually finding some comfort in a top about thirty yards from my blind. The doe stayed there all morning. It was one of those times you never forget. I put the turkey call down and simply shared the woods with the animal for the rest of the morning, feeling much obliged when it got up and left a few minutes before I had to.

Finally, after backtracking a couple of times, I'm at the birch stand. The three trunks twist crookedly to the sky, like an arthritic, weathered hand that has seen too much life. Fifteen feet up the largest trunk, the flashlight illuminates a four-foot section that is

146

perfectly vertical. That's where I always hang the stand. Placing my backpack and the stand on the ground, I pull the screw-in steps out of the pack. I look disdainfully down at the handful of innocent-looking steel steps. Getting them screwed into the tree is the hardest part of the whole setup. Screwing the first step in, I'm holding the flashlight in my mouth when I notice something surprising. Right next to it, only two inches away on the flaky, white bark, is the old tree-step hole. I move the step into the dark old scar and easily twist it into place. Shining the beam up the trunk, I see the staggered black dots marking the way, all the way up to where the stand goes. I'm surprised the holes are still there. It's been at least three years—maybe four—since I last hunted here. Each step goes in easily with only the smallest effort.

Sitting in the stand in the dark, I feel the slightest hint of a breeze in my face. The snow is supposed to come at daylight and the wind is predicted to kick up later in the morning. I'm hoping it waits.

I hear a pack of coyotes yipping on the far ridge.

Lost in thoughts and memories, I am surprised when the sun comes up. It shines fiercely in a tiny strip of clear sky on the eastern horizon, illuminating the underside of the massive gray storm front with hot red light. The sun has no chance to warm the hill before it rises up and disappears behind the gray clouds. I don't know it now, but the sun has made its final appearance for a week. The sky again darkens, threatening to turn to night all over again.

A moment later, I wonder if I really saw the sun at all.

When the snow comes, I'm amazed at its intensity. There are none of the light flakes that normally precede a storm. There's no warning. At precisely 8:00 A.M. the gloomy skies simply open up. The wind that was supposed to wait until later also comes up, driving the heavy snow sideways. Settling my back into the white birch, I watch the big flakes come down, snow piling up on me and all around me. My face hurts as the new snow is driven into it by the harsh wind. I can stand it for a while. Since visibility is down to about five yards, I don't see any reason to sit out the morning here. I try brushing the snow off my bow, soaking my glove in the process. My nocked arrow even has a half-inch of accumulation down its length. Taking the arrow off the string, I shake the snow off it. A few more minutes, I tell myself, then I'm out of here.

Suddenly there's a deer below me.

Looking down at its wide back and big, wide rack, I have no idea where it came from. Quickly nocking the arrow again, I try to deaden the snap with my gloved fingers. The deer pauses only for a moment below the stand, then walks around behind me. I want to rise from the seat and turn around but have no idea how close it is. My mind races. I forget the cold, forget the snow. I forget everything except the sight of the buck.

A few minutes pass—or perhaps only a few seconds—but suddenly there is a big disturbance behind me. Even with the howling wind and banging tree limbs, I hear the unmistakable sound of leaves being pawed. Daring to crane my neck around, all I see (other than snow) are leaves and dirt flying. I can't see the buck, but its fountain of debris rises fifteen feet in the air. I slowly rise, amazed at the quantity of the snow that has piled up on the stand at my feet. There is a slight crunch as I shift my feet on the tiny platform. I freeze. Luckily, the sound is carried off on the wind.

Wildly pawing a scrape, the buck has its back to me. Making low grunts as it furiously tears at the white ground, it seems to be angry with the snow for covering its handiwork. It pauses, looking left and then right, perhaps sensing someone watching it. Apparently satisfied it is safe, the big buck resumes ripping up the earth. Its dark coat stands out in stark contrast to the white ground.

Still facing the tree, I'm in a fairly awkward position if I should need to draw my bow. . . . Suddenly the buck is moving quickly to the right, taking fast and purposeful steps. About fifteen yards out, it's broadside to me. When it passes behind a double-trunked, six-inch birch, I draw the bow quickly, somehow managing not to bang the tree.

I see plenty of these guys—except during deer season.

In the second it takes me to draw, the deer stops, having either heard or smelled me. It's locked up behind the tree. Noticing the pattern of the snowflakes blowing from me to it, I realize it's scented me.

I wait for it to take one more step, and the weight of the bow tugs at my frozen muscles. I see its muzzle and the front edge of its antlers as it turns its head from side to side.

Turning ninety degrees behind the tree, the buck faces me. One eye and one antler are all I can see. It's looking right at me, or perhaps right under me. Either way, it's got me. I practiced all summer at holding the bow at full draw, but the practice doesn't pay on this miserable, cold day. My left hand wavers, and I watch helplessly as my right hand moves forward to join it. The buck doesn't hesitate a second, racing off across the open meadow into the blizzard. About sixty yards out, it stops and turns, looking right at me again. That sight of him, only barely visible through the snow, makes me shiver.

I'm shivering. I snap my head up, confused and expecting to see snow, but there is none. There's nothing but the sea of amber beech leaves and gray saplings cut here and there by the wayward brook. I try hard to remember the dream.

Was it a dream? No. It really happened. Today, however, it's just a dream. I try to remember how many years ago I saw that buck. Maybe three. Maybe five. It doesn't matter. That's how time is here on the hill.

I look around the woods, then close my eyes, trying to revive the dream; sorry it's gone. A moment later, it fades back into its proper place with all the other memories that have been born in these woods. Like the brook now flooding the woods, that deep river of memories sometimes breaks its bank, showing up unexpectedly and stirring up the landscape.

My nap has lasted less than ten minutes, but I'm suddenly wide awake, thankful I secured my safety belt before dozing off. There's a squirrel on the ground twenty yards to my right, gathering something off the carpet of leaves, probably fallen beechnuts. I wonder if it is my squirrel, and I picture it running across my lap while I was off in dreamland. The squirrel suddenly chatters and races for a nearby oak tree, disappearing into a long crease in its trunk. If that was my squirrel, it would've raced for my tree.

Looking back over my shoulder to where the squirrel dived into the tree, I'm shocked when I turn back around to the sight of a deer trotting down the trail toward me. Through the saplings, I see four brown legs.

Rising carefully to my feet, I hope my motion is hidden by the trees in front of me. Still coming steadily, the deer isn't trotting now, just walking. When it disappears behind the last clump of trees before the opening, I pull my bow back. The arrow makes a slight hiss on the rest and I cringe, but the deer doesn't hear it over the water. When it comes out from behind the tree, I see two little spike antlers on its head. It pauses in the opening, perhaps sensing me. Since it is only ten yards from me, this would be the perfect shot. If I hadn't already filled my buck tag, the arrow would have been sent. Giving me a good view, it turns this way and that in front of me. Still concerned with something behind it, the deer throws one more glance back over his shoulder before trotting on down through the spruces and out of sight.

My heart pounds hard as I lower the bow with shaky hands. My senses are on full alert and a shudder racks my body. The adrenaline pours through my veins, and the rush is incredible. I concentrate hard on calming myself, deciding to sit down and take a deep breath. I'm halfway sitting when the next deer pops into the clearing. The little doe is in front of me before I know it. Also stopping in the clearing, it sniffs the precise spot where the buck stopped. Again raising my bow, I don't draw. It's tiny, probably this year's fawn. Carefully watching the trail behind it, I hope a bigger doe might be following. At one point, the deer looks right up at me. I avoid its eyes as it bobs its head, trying to make something concrete out of the dark blob in the tree. A stray breeze carries my scent down to it, and the doe suddenly trots off with its tail flicking up and down, legs stiff. Long after it's out of sight, I'm still flushed with the excitement of the two close encounters. At noon, the fact that I'm in a good spot is obvious, but the water is once again driving me mad. With some trepidation, I pull my stand down, vowing to remember the spot and come back here next year if the woods are drier.

Sometimes the does are craftier than the bucks. . . .

At John's request, I pick him up on the way out of the woods. He's shaking his head as he walks down out of the pine stand to meet me. A doe had come up the trail passing perfectly broadside to his stand. Pausing behind the berry bush, it wouldn't come out, playing peek-a-boo with him and finally disappearing up the hill without presenting a shot.

"If that damn bush wasn't there, I would've had her," he says, clearly disappointed. As we sit and eat our lunch on Doc's back fence, I don't bother to mention that I picked that spot for his stand because of the bush. Some things are best left unsaid.

Dad emerges from the orchard just as John is heading back up to his stand. He's shaking his head, too. He missed a doe early on. With the deer standing broadside at ten yards, he was sick as he watched his arrow bury itself in the ground under it. John and I harass him, telling him the deer was probably too small for him to get a good aiming point. He doesn't think we are all that funny.

After lunch, I still can't decide where to hunt. John and Dad have long since retreated back to the woods, and I'm still on the stone fence, pondering. The drive to hunt every available second is not there for me. If I don't fill my doe tag, I'll still have it in a few weeks when we're back for rifle season. There's no need to knock myself out trying to arrow another deer. My eyes close again, and I'm once again thinking of the stand in my dream. It really has been a long time since I hunted up there.

The decision is made.

I stand up from the fence, the breath catches in my chest. In the field behind Doc's house are five deer. This is too good to be true. Two of the does stand precisely where my buck was a few weeks ago when I first saw him. The other three, also does, munch on clover in a wet patch near the center of the field. I can't believe my luck. Grabbing my bow, I start the crawl across Doc's back lawn.

This is getting too familiar.

Reaching the stone fence, I spot the deer feeding together in a tight group at the far end of the field, out of sight of Doc's house. Crouching low, I trot the length of the field, hidden by the stone fence and a cooperative breeze. Sneaking several peeks over the stones, I notice the deer angling toward the old cattle gate. After a short dash, I take up position next to a large spruce tree. With shaking hands, I snap an arrow onto the string.

I let the moment pass, and my next peek over the gate tells me I've been had. Two of the bigger does are facing squarely at my position, heads up, ears forward. The other three feed peacefully between them, but this pair stares right at me. Ducking my head back behind the fence slowly, I'm sure the does have spotted my movement. I look at my watch, letting a full ten minutes pass before looking over the fence again. When I do, the five deer have moved to the back edge of the field. I am not surprised. Though they are feeding calmly again, not a moment passes that one of the bigger does doesn't turn around, looking suspiciously over its shoulder in my direction. There's no way they'll come back.

Having nothing to lose, I take the grunt call from around my neck. Laying the bow down, I cradle the long tube in both hands, raising it to the sky as if I were bugling for elk. "*Waaaaaaaaaa. Waaaaaaaaaaaa.*" All five heads snap up in unison, looking directly at me. But they quickly resume feeding. Two hundred yards away, I'm not worried about spooking them so I call again. "*Waaaaaaaaaa. Waaaaaaaa. Waaaaaaaaaa.*"

This time a few of the heads turn toward me and a few turn back toward the woods. Three of the deer, the older does, dash into the cover of the spruces. Two of the younger ones consider me a while longer. Unexpectedly, a spike buck jumps the fence, coming into the field as the two remaining does head for cover. Turning its head frantically around, it listens for the source of the call. I oblige it with a soft, seductive doe bleat, then freeze when the buck stares in my direction. The rut has been going strong for a week, and the younger bucks don't get many breeding opportunities, usually being driven off by the larger bucks. This little buck's sexual frustration nearly leads to its demise. Casting a quick look back toward the woods, it checks to make certain some big buck isn't sneaking up, preparing to chase it off. Then, dashing headlong across the field, the deer runs straight at me. I've never seen anything like it. High noon and the buck runs across an open field. Beckoned by the three-dollar grunt tube, he's certainly not thinking with his brain. Instead of veering through the cattle gate, it leaps the stone fence like Superman, landing broadside twenty yards from me. Even though my scent blows toward it, the buck is still looking for its sweetheart. Only partially concealed by the tree from this angle, I wave my right arm to attract its attention. It steps toward me! Not wishing to be mounted on my lunch break, I stand from my crouch and yell, "Boo!" The buck vaults across the stone fence, but pauses on the other side to get one last look at me. There's fire in its eyes, and I'm not sure I like the look it gives me before racing across the field, finally disappearing into the spruces on the other side.

The afternoon passes slowly in the old birch stand. It's nice to be back in this desolate stretch of woods, but the excitement of this morning's dreams and memories is nowhere to be found as I ride the slowly rocking tree. All around me, the woods sway to the gentle wind. Around four, a glimpse of brown through the thick blowdowns catches my attention and I slowly rise to my feet. About a hundred yards out, a small buck is sneaking through the woods. Picking up my grunt call, I let go with a low "*urrrrrp.*" There is a slight hitch in the buck's step, but it continues quickly on, not even glancing in my direction.

Dusk comes slowly, and I'm a little disappointed in the bland happenings of the afternoon. I shouldn't have expected them to compare to this morning's vivid dreams and memories. I close my eyes one more time, hoping for the dreams to come.

All that comes is sunset.

November 11—Monday

Snow falls heavily all around me, muting the sounds of the woods and quickly covering my tracks to the stand. It's long since covered the tracks of the buck that came through an hour or so before I arrived. Its tracks coursed directly up the hill, stopping only to paw at two scrapes not far from my stand. The deer made a circle around the ground blind I put together after dark last night in preparation for rifle season. Then, unbelievably, its tracks snaked around the base of the three birch trees holding my stand. I followed the tracks on the way up, fascinated. It's as if it backtracked every move I made when I left last night. Had it been watching me?

The morning again reminds me of the big buck that got away. This morning is identical to that one. The problem with hunting is the amount of stuff you bring to the woods with you. Not the kind in your backpack—that's easy enough to carry—but the kind in your head. The morning is peaceful and perfect, and naturally my mind races. The nagging worries of everyday life stand out in sharp contrast to the melancholy woods. I think of the trailer behind my truck, already packed and ready to go. What a hellishly long trip we have ahead of us. This snow won't help. I hope the transmission—which has been grinding incessantly— holds out.

The woods become full of ghosts. Ghosts of the people who used to live here, the ghosts of departed friends. Ghosts of former friends whom I've lost touch with that might as well be a world away. The ghosts talk to me, crowding the stand, bullying their way from the back of my mind right up to the front.

Enough! Picking up my binoculars, I carefully scan the woods one more time.

Walking back downhill takes longer today because of the tree stand strapped to my back. I'm kicking myself for leaving early, knowing I'll regret it months from now. Halfway down, I have an idea. Dropping the pack and stand, I turn around and walk back up the hill. Passing the birch trees, I search the ground for the faint deer tracks, now buried by snow. They appear as slight depressions. I'll be up here on opening day of rifle season in the new ground blind, and I want to know where this buck went. Its trail stays straight across the meadow, leading directly away from my tree stand. But a hundred yards out, entering the beech saplings on the far side of the meadow, I find three small trees rubbed at the edge of the woods. The buck's trail then makes an abrupt right, following the edge of the saplings back down in front of my stand. Another slight angle to the right makes it clear that the buck that made these tracks is the same one I saw this morning. The faint, buried tracks end in a fresh deer bed. I sit down in the bed, facing the way the deer was facing.

What I see is the tree I just left.

The buck was watching me, at least this morning. The bed smells of deer musk, a wild smell, strange to my nose. Out the downhill side of the bed, a single set of fresh tracks, still mostly untouched by the falling snow, winds past my stand. The deer must have been lying here all morning, watching me come in and climb the tree in the dark. Finally, it just got bored with watching me— or had someplace else to be—and carefully skirted the tree stand, knowing I was there. That's why it wasn't fooled by the grunt call.

Checking my new ground blind one more time, I find some more fresh deer tracks on the nearby trails. Scanning the woods,

I make a mental picture of the place so I can walk to it in the darkness of opening morning. I can't wait.

Doc Campbell meets me in the driveway, disappointed when I tell him we've only managed to remove one of his shrubbery-eating deer so far this year. Though I haven't talked to him in months, the conversation is easy and quiet, the friendship mutual. Before getting into his jeep to drive into town, he asks me to clean some more of his deer out during rifle season. Part of the way down the driveway, he backs up and rolls down his window.

"Back at the Maple Pond, three deer were right out in the open by the water a few minutes ago," he says, with a gleam in his eye. He lifts his hands, drawing back an imagined bow. There is a wide grin on his face as he drives away.

Tossing the stand on the trailer, I start taking off my hunting clothes. When my down coat slides off, exposing my arm and my watch, I gulp. It's only nine-thirty. We weren't supposed to meet until noon. The ghosts chased me off the stand even earlier than I thought. Trying to make good use of the time, I reorganize the truck, carefully tying down all the gear on the trailer. It's amazing the amount of bulky equipment it took for two bow hunters to hunt for a few short days. There are stands and bow cases, two shotgun cases, countless backpacks and tackle boxes, sleeping bags, and duffel bags. It was a fairly organized pile when we left last week, but now it resembles a sporting goods store after a bombing. Getting it back in order is a good expenditure of my excess energy. Once its done, I look at my watch again. Only a half-hour has passed.

Thinking about the Maple Pond, I once again dig into the pile. Pulling my bow case from under the pile of duffel bags, I curse as the back of the truck rearranges itself once again. Walking up past the house, I snap an arrow onto the string and pull down my face mask. The little corridor of white pines leading up to the pond is grouse heaven. Although I jump at the sound, I'm not surprised when two birds flush across the trail in front of me. I am surprised, however; when I look in the direction they flushed from and spot another grouse hiding against the base of the tree.

Trying to move easily, I draw the bow, placing the sight on the bird's body. There are a lot of branches between the bird and me, and the shot is over thirty yards. It's hard to tell if the arrow hits the bird, and I feel a slight bit of disappointment when the bird flushes straight up, wings thundering. The disappointment quickly turns to glee when the bird crumples to the ground.

I can't believe it! The arrow, laced with feathers and a few drops of blood, is stuck in the base of a pine. The grouse is right next to the arrow, having crashed right back where it took off from. Laughing loudly, I know how much luck was involved. Of course, I'll never admit that.

When Dad comes out of the woods, he looks tired and ready to go. Dropping his heavy ladder stand on the ground next to the truck, he says he saw some deer this morning, but none close enough to shoot at. "See anything?" he asks.

Tossing his stand in the trailer, I hold up the grouse.

"You're supposed to get a doe!" he says, smiling.

"Anyone can hit a deer—well, almost anyone—but it takes skill to shoot a bird."

"I can see it's going to be a long ride home."

November 13—The Last Rooster

Waist deep in the grass covering the old vineyard road, I plod on. On the other side of the hedgerow, Brian has Ted hanging on his boots. It's been a long morning, with several miles of walking producing only one flush—a hen. There is no wind, and between the sunny spells, flurries dance through the air. The two inches of snow blanketing the ground give away the secret haunts of rabbits and pheasants, but the owners of the tracks have been especially evasive today. The snow has made the usually rough walk through the vineyard even harder and after a few hours we're ready to quit.

Suddenly, Maggie is snorting. She doesn't seem focused, but she's moving jerkily back and forth.

"There's rabbit tracks here."

As she pokes her head into the long grass to my left, a rabbit promptly shoots out the other side of the clump, popping out only a foot away. The cottontail turns to zip back between Brian and me. I shoot first, blasting the snow behind the rabbit. Before I can shoot again, Brian hammers it.

"You can hit them in snow, too?"

Tired, Brian and I would probably have quit shortly, but shooting the rabbit suddenly has our blood flowing again. We decide to go back to Ransomville and give the place that disappointed us on opening day one last chance. The walk back past the corn is longer than ever, but the little bit of snow covers the mud and our feet aren't sucked in on every step. One of the hedgerows dividing the corn suddenly attracts the dogs' attention. Brian and I spot a gray squirrel trying to escape to the other end of the hedgerow, where it meets the hardwoods. Caught out in the open, it can't escape except with speed and luck. Just before it gets clear of the row and into the woods, its luck runs out.

Since there's only a day or two of pheasant hunting left, I let the dogs run wild in the corn. Brian spots a big set of pheasant tracks crossing out of the corn and into the ditch on our left. I point the dogs at the tracks. The dogs snort and sniff madly as they follow the bird's route. The tracks must be fresh. I wonder if we pushed it out of the corn. The dogs concentrate their efforts in a thick thornbush tangle between a huge culvert and the ditch. Looking down into the deep ditch,

I'm pretty sure I've spotted fresh tracks coming out the other side of the tangle.

"Oh crap!" I hear from behind me.

Whirling around just in time to see the shot, I hear the rooster's cackle. Brian's first shot misses. At the second one, the bird dives into the long grass on the opposite side of the ditch.

"Good shot!" I yell.

We wish we could run across and make sure the bird is dead, but we can't. The water is deep and we'll have to go around the Culvert Bridge. Absorbed with locating the bird, the dogs didn't see the flush. At the sound of the shots, they vault out of the ditch. I point them across and they dive in enthusiastically. Quickly swimming across, they begin working the long grass furiously. The chase is on, the scent is fresh, and they bounce around insanely trying to locate the rooster.

As Brian and I stand on the Culvert Bridge, a rooster—a very healthy rooster—flushes from under my dogs' noses. Following it with a rapid shot, I miss. Brian and I debate whether or not that was his rooster. The one he shot at appeared dead as it crashed, but appearances aren't everything. The other problem is that the dogs are still concentrating on the grass instead of being interested in the flushing bird. Brian and I run to the grassy patch, helping the dogs search for the fallen bird. Walking back and forth, we crisscross the area, peering into every clump of grass we can find. After a dozen trips through, even the dogs lose interest. If the scent were still strong, they would stay with it, and that's not happening.

We spend the remaining daylight in the corn, and the dogs get back on scent but run us in circles. I know it's the rooster. I just know it. But it won't show itself, or even have the decency to flush out of range. It just runs us in more circles until it is too dark to see.

November 14—The Last Rooster, Again

There is no way we're going to let it get away.

When I meet Brian at the cornfield after work once again, there is only an hour or so before dark. Quickly pushing the dogs

"Ringneck was here," say the lines and tracks in the snow.

through the grassy patch, we plow headlong into the cornfield. Immediately picking up fresh bird scent, the dogs are off on another romp through the corn. Again, Brian and I are in muddy, hot pursuit. We find the rooster's tracks—where they aren't covered by dog tracks. Once again, we are going in circles. After half an hour, Brian and I just stop exasperated, letting the dogs run it around us.

This is frustrating. This is an exceptionally smart bird.

Panting heavily, Maggie and Ted look at us peculiarly as they appear in and out of the corn rows. This bird is really pissing them off. After another ten minutes of running up and down the corn rows, we hear the dogs crossing the corn back toward the hedgerow. Running across the rows, I exit the corn just in time to see the rooster flush over the open field. I am stunned when it makes an impossible turn, evading the bead of my shotgun, which swings clumsily past it. Flying back over the heads of the dogs, it lands just inside the corn. The dogs eagerly give chase.

It's as if the bird wants to be chased. He could easily have flown to the next hedgerow but elected to dash back into the security of the corn. I bet it thinks it could outrun these stupid dogs all day if it wanted to. And it's probably right.

The sun comes down on the last day of pheasant hunting with us chasing the rooster through the corn, trying to no avail to make it flush. This is one smart bird. The dogs trail on our heels all the way back to the truck, exhausted and whipped by the bird and the harsh cornstalks. We've been beaten by the rooster. The last bird of the year is the first to whip us. There is no regret, only laughter, as we follow the lights from the houses back to the parking lot. Already thinking ahead, I can't wait until next year. As if in answer, a rooster cackles far behind us.

Deer Season

The season here is never wasted.
Each moment is savored, each day appreciated.
Each year, these mountains share something.
The nature of the gift, always unique.

November 17—Walkabout

The ground blind looks good. There's no snow around to tell me if the buck has been back in the past week, but the two nearby scrapes have been freshly pawed. I *know* he's here. John looks at the blind as Howard gives it his seal. My brother-in-law, Steve, checks out a nearby trail. Ushering them away from the area quickly, I have no desire to leave our scent all over the area the day before rifle season, but I don't really mind. This is tradition. Walking around together on the Sunday before opening day, we help one another set up and select places from which to hunt. Since none of us live around here anymore, the opportunity to get out and see the countryside, to experience the peace and beauty of the woods, is worth any chance we take of spooking the deer. The question of who is going to hunt where never ends. Some years, the debate rages on into the early morning of opening day. The problem isn't that there are too many of us, not by a long shot. The real dilemma is that there are several good places to hunt and it's difficult to narrow them down. I'm set, but the other guys are still pondering.

Up the mountain from my blind is the wildest piece of land on the property. There are bear caves where giant hemlocks reach dizzying heights. Three brooks splash their way down through a beautiful array of boulders and waterfalls. There are more turkeys there than anywhere else on earth. The deer are plentiful but more secretive than the ones living on the main part of the property around Doc's house. The place has been pretty much forsaken by our group of hunters, simply for the difficulties of making the long hike in and getting seated before daylight—not to mention the exhausting drag if you shoot a deer.

Howard planned to hunt the pasture, where he'd been clearing brush when Dad and I were bowhunting. Unfortunately, he found out this morning that the new caretaker told his wife she could hunt there. Howard wisely and graciously conceded the area to her, despite all the work he'd put into clearing lanes. Now he wants to hunt the upper side on opening day, something he hasn't done in several years. Hiking up the south property line, the four of us follow the remnants of an old barbed wire fence. I can't even count the times I've been turned around up here thankful when this old fence came into view. It's the only direct line between the deep woods and the road. All the trails snake and angle and look the same, so the fence is a lifesaver. Crossing the last brook, we make the steep climb up to the back line, the western edge of Doc's property. Huge boulders, some the size of houses, lie strewn about between the ancient hemlocks and beeches. Covered in green moss, they look like the forgotten toys of some mythical giant. Sitting for a few moments, we silently take in the view downhill into the creek bottom. Finding a flat rock where I can sit and catch my breath, I suddenly realize I'm sitting precisely where I shot the big doe last year.

I can still picture the day. Howard, hunting the opposite side of the ravine, spooked about twenty deer and they all streamed downhill in front of me. I simply picked the biggest one, laid my cross hairs against its chest, and watched it tumble into the dark shade of the hemlocks. The shot hadn't seemed hard, but I hadn't had time to think about it. When I went to retrieve the deer, I paced it off at 120 yards. It was the longest shot at a moving deer I've ever made. Congratulating myself about the monstrous doe, I wasn't thinking of the drag. It was exhausting, and the sun had been down a long time when we finally reached the road. . . .

Finding a small finger of ground high above the creek bottom, Howard begins piling up flat rocks on which to sit. The view from the knoll is spectacular. We each sit on his rock seat, approving of it before we begin the long trek back down.

In the evening, after dinner with Howard Sr. and Myrtle, we all gather in the basement, making our final preparations. Loading our coats and vests, we try to remember everything. There are gloves and knives, drag ropes and candy bars, tissues and wads of toilet paper (oh God, please don't let me forget toilet paper). After our coats are stuffed, we check our rifles. Howard, in keeping with tradition, holds up a single .30-06 cartridge.

"I've got my one shot, but I think I'm gonna have to pack an extra since I've got a doe permit this year," he says with a gleam in his eye.

We remind the one-shot wonder about having to shoot a buck twice. Grumbling something about the wind, he looks down at his yellow-and-green box of shells and begins counting aloud. ". . . seven, eight, nine . . . well, assuming that they give out doe permits for the next few years, I shouldn't have to buy shells until the year 2000," he says, the wicked grin back on his face. We all erupt in laughter.

The lights go out early, but the talk and excitement go on well into the night. One by one, the other hunters, arranged around the basement floor in their sleeping bags, drop out of the conversation. I'm left staring up at the black ceiling, impatiently waiting for sunrise.

Sleep does not come easily.

November 18—Opening Day

The blind seems cramped. Shifting, I try to make my legs fit without hitting the pile of branches in front of me, knowing it's my nervous energy—not the close quarters—making me fidget.

The months I have dreamed about this come rushing upon me. The satisfying feeling of finally *being* here is only slightly overwhelmed by the excitement and anxiety. The sunrise won't come fast enough.

White-tailed doe in the morning light. I can't think of anything more beautiful.

It won't be long before Howard makes his way up the hill. He doesn't like sitting in the dark, preferring to still-hunt to his rock pile on the upper side. Planning to pass within a few hundred yards of my stand right at daylight, he hopes anything he spooks might run past me. I think we have had even more success over the years with these little two-man plans than we ever do during the big drives.

I can't wait for the drives. We usually sit in our stands until late morning and then put on some small drives, finally sitting out the last hours of daylight back in our stands. I like sitting and waiting, but the drives are the centerpiece of our deer hunt. They are when all of us, old friends and new, come together with a common purpose. Plans are laid. Friends are made and remade. The excitement of our deer drives rivals even the most successful day sitting on a stand. There is something primal, tribal, about pushing deer down through the valleys to the waiting standers. The newer guys always want to sit, but those of us who have been hunting here a few years know sometimes the most exciting place to be is walking down through the dark places, with the deer crashing out ahead.

As I suddenly picture Howard Sr. and me walking down through the bowl on his last hunt, a ripple of sadness passes through me. How must he feel sitting down in the house this morning? He was up when we left, which was ridiculously early. How will he feel when the first shots start echoing down from the mountain? Anytime I start worrying that this season, or the others, has become an obsession, that I'm expending too much time and energy, I need only look at Greta's grandfather and be reminded that one day I'll also no longer be able to climb the hill. Sitting here in the cold, cramped blind, I'm aware that every sense is on full alert, and every sound makes me twitch with excitement. I feel as if I couldn't be more alive.

Obsession has its merits.

Around seven, my nerves have settled and the woods around me have grown light under a gray dawn. The sound of crunching leaves suddenly sets me off, jangling my nerves once again. An old stone fence runs parallel to my blind, and the noise is coming from the other side of it. There are two big openings in the stones where the two deer trails cross. The far one, fifty yards away, is where my first buck took its last steps. The crunching passes the first opening, and suddenly a deer's head appears, bobbing up and down over the stones and angling uphill toward the closer opening. The deer drops out of sight behind a higher section of the stone fence and I raise my rifle, resting the scope's cross hairs across the opening. This is the moment I've dreamed of for nearly a year. The mountains all around are suddenly popping with the sounds of rifle shots as people gather their venison early on this magical morning. The deer never appears in the opening, but I don't hear it leave the area. Torturing myself, I imagine it bedded down just the other side of the stone fence. Trying to drive the image from my mind, I know it doesn't matter whether it's there or not. But the thought just won't go away. What if it's a big buck just lying there, unaware, a few scant yards from me? After giving the deer a full hour, I rise with painful slowness to a low crouch. My cold back screams and begs to be straightened as I take the eleven steps from the blind to the stone fence. Carefully rising and peeking over, I see nothing but the steep hill, painted in gray and amber. A loud crunching from behind me makes me cringe.

Caught *again*.

The line of turkeys appears on the far side of the ground blind. Yanking my face mask down again, I sit against the stone fence. Trying to be quiet, I plunk down rather loudly in the crisp beech leaves. The turkeys pause, but only briefly, and then are suddenly pouring around the ground blind, passing on both sides of me. The nearest bird jumps up on the stone fence only ten feet from me.

One by one they hop on the fence, splatting down on the opposite side before continuing noisily on down the hill. Using the cover of the turkeys' noise, I slip quickly back into the ground blind.

The shooting on the surrounding hills has tapered off, but each time a shot goes off nearby, I wonder if it's one of my friends. The echo up and down through the hills and valleys makes pinpointing the source impossible. Around ten, a single crunch in the woods behind me makes me nearly jump out of my skin. Having my back to an enormous boulder, I have to peek ever so carefully around it to see where the deer is coming from. The sleeve of my coat catches on some unseen branch, which whips back with a loud crack. Sitting back in the blind, I try to let any damage I've done subside before peeking around the rock again. When I finally do, I see a figure in red plaid standing there, smoking a cigarette, leaning against a tree and watching me with amusement.

Howard. He was supposed to pick me up on the way out, but he's early. I'm relieved when he holds two fingers above his head, signaling a spike. It's going to be a long drag, but how big can a spike be?

It's *huge.*

Deer Driving

Static crackles over my radio. "Joel, are you in?" Howard asks.

"I'm in. Mike, you in?"

"Let's go," Mike says, the excitement in his voice coming in clearly through my headset.

The temperature in the shade of the hemlocks is ten degrees colder than up on the hillside. The runways parallel the bubbling brook, crossing and recrossing it here and there. We move quietly, since we know the deer can be pushed more easily if they don't know exactly where we are. Every now and then, one of us asks the others to whistle as we sneak through the dark valley, to keep everyone moving in a straight line. The only one of the standers with a radio is John, and he is quiet, listening excitedly as we move slowly toward his position. Occasionally, the deer come out far ahead of the drivers, moving cautiously. John knows better than to give away his location at the big maple tree by talking to us.

Realizing I'm moving too fast, I stop for a moment and sit, waiting for Howard and Mike to catch up. The woods are thick here, and the two little apple trees to the west still hold a fair amount of fruit. It's a good area. The first to spot a deer is Howard.

"Four of them, right in front of me."

Somehow, Mike doesn't see the deer as they cross the brook in front of him and climb the bank in front of me. It looks like three large deer and one smaller one, but they are moving fast through the timber and I get only a glimpse. As the deer race up the hill, I alter my course to try and intercept them. They are long gone before I get there. They've crossed the road and gone up the hill toward my ground blind, successfully escaping the drive. I radio the other guys and tell them we lost at least four deer. We're only eighty yards from the standers, and the chatter picks up on the headsets. Howard and I discuss the next drive. John asks how close we are to coming out. The tension that filled the air at the beginning of the drive subsides as we make plans for the rest of the day. I'm looking down at a fresh set of tracks when something grabs my attention. When I snap my head up, a small buck is standing in an opening about fifty yards from me, staring at me. Below me, Mike is still moving, oblivious.

"John," I say breathlessly, "there's a spike right in between me and you."

"*Shoot* if you can!"

"He's right between us! I can't shoot."

The spike doesn't hesitate long, splashing back down into the brook, in front of Mike, who is fighting the thick brush. It disappears on Howard's side of the brook, but he hasn't seen it yet. I'm nearly within sight of John when a single shot thunders from the other side of the brook. Once again, the voices in my headset come alive with excitement.

Kneeling over the buck when we come out, Albert is all smiles. Instead of sticking with the cover of the hemlocks, the spike had raced out across the orchard, running directly at Al, who was sitting on a log-splitter, next to a pile of cut wood. He says the deer was so close that he could barely fit it in his scope.

"*Another* spike," Howard says, shaking his head.

Dusk creeps in as the land is washed clean by rain. Crows caw around us, enjoying their spoils. The rain soaks through my coat as light vanishes into dark. The branches of the spruce that protected me from the rain can no longer hold away the water, sending rivulets down my neck and back. The excitement of the day fades into a melancholy sadness, not for lack of success. The sadness is in the knowledge that one more day has come and gone here on the hill, never to be seen again except in dreams and memories. I think of Howard Sr. and what he wouldn't give to be sitting up here in the rain like a fool with the rest of us. It's hard to feel time passing here in the protection of the ancient trees. Maybe that's why we keep coming back.

November 19—Success, in Any Form

A single shot rings out, sounding like it came from the orchard, but I can't be sure. I have my hands full. About an hour before dark a large, dark doe and several smaller deer suddenly appeared at the pines in the back of the field. Sitting here all afternoon, I've been fighting intense boredom. Now I can't slow my heart rate.

The deer hesitate only for a moment before crossing out into the open, heading for a dark green patch of clover growing over a spring. Nestling back against the willow tree at the edge of the pond, I try to disappear. The .308 resting across my lap slowly comes up to my knee. The doe, across the pond and quite a way out in the field, is 120 yards from me. It's not an extremely long shot, but the deer's coming closer, so I wait.

Kicking its legs jubilantly, one of the younger deer has obviously not been spooked by all the day's shooting. In fact, all the deer are calm as they browse the field. Turning broadside to me, the big doe walks slowly across the field. Popping open the scope caps, I wait for the right moment. I dial the scope up a notch or two, and the cross hairs fall into place on her shoulder. Suddenly, the doe is staring down the scope tube at me. Somehow, it's locked onto me. Quickly looking back toward the pines, it stomps its foot. I hurriedly resettle the cross hairs on the deer. Cocking the hammer, I gently pull the trigger. The shot feels perfect. After the rifle roars, I'm astonished to see the doe still standing broadside as I chamber another shell. Catching sight of my motion, it's off, along with its companions, disappearing into the refuge of the pines. I look down at my .308, which I shot and sighted religiously all summer. It's never failed me before. The lone eye of the scope looks up at me balefully.

This is the second opportunity I've blown today. Early in the morning John and I hiked into "The Bowl" and sat for a few hours. The Bowl is a hemlock-lined area of Doc's property that starts in the pasture, then angles steeply downhill into the dark hemlock woods. Descending into darkness, the woods form a cup shape—a bowl. Early this morning John and I decided the shelter of the hemlocks would be a good place to wait out the morning's rain. Dropping him off on the property line, I hiked for fifteen minutes in the dark, finally finding a huge old hemlock with branches that swept nearly to the ground. Nestled in under the branches as the sky lightened, I found I had a rather commanding view of the valley. Almost as soon as I could see, I spotted a deer in The Bowl. From my high vantage point, it was merely a moving blob of brown with a long neck. It was following the creek, and I hoped it would eventually make its way up to John, who was sitting on one of the main runways. An hour later, my entire body was soaked and the "waterproof" hat on my head felt like a sponge. The rain came in sheets. The wind, too, had found its way into the valley, chilling my wet body. I couldn't stop picturing the woodstove back at Howard and Myrtle's.

Just when the rain was at its heaviest, three deer appeared below me 150 yards away, moving steadily along the brook. Their

Hiding in plain sight. A white-tailed doe stands motionless.

hooves made no sound in the soft hemlock needles—at least none that the rain would allow me to hear. When they moved past me into a clearing, I saw they were three large does. Once they slipped out of sight over a small knoll, I decided to follow them. Slipping— sometimes quite literally—down over the mossy rocks, I immediately picked up their faint hoofprints in the hemlock needles. Having found where they crossed the brook, I paused, just peeking my head over the bank. They were nowhere in sight. Crossing the ten-foot-wide brook, the deer joined up with a major runway. I thought the deer had probably just finished feeding in the orchard and were headed toward the spruces, where they could lay down to chew their cud out of the rain. I hurried my pace, following the deer trail. It dipped down into another brook, which I jumped across. Racing up the opposite bank, I hoped to catch the trio of does before they got to the spruces. Moving quickly was easy on the quiet carpet of needles. It was also a mistake. The three deer were bedded on the opposite side of the brook. When they stood up, I noticed the closest was only twenty-five yards away. Before I could get my gun off my shoulder, the three made the final hundred-yard push up into the spruces, white tails waving and taunting as they bounded up the hill out of sight.

The rest of the morning was eventless, giving me plenty of time to kick myself.

Waiting a while before walking out, I check the field for any sign I hit the doe. The mossy grass is wet, and I quickly find the tracks where the deer stood when I shot. The large tracks stand out in the soft ground. Finding where it slowed to jump the old wire strands, I also observe where it walked into the dense pines. Trailing it through the crusty snow that remains in the shade of the pines, I follow it until I'm convinced it isn't hit. Hanging my head in disappointment, I know I did everything right except hit the deer. I just wish Howard and

Albert hadn't been at the other end of the field watching the whole thing.

As I emerge from the spruces, their voices fill the headset of my radio, teasing me about the miss. They'd been watching the doe, too, talking quietly into their radios as the deer entered the field. I had hoped the group of deer would head *their* way, so they wouldn't have to watch me shoot. They watched the deer through their scopes as I shot and missed, getting a clear view of the whole sorry show. Oh, well. I'm going to hear about this one for a long time.

Hiking back to the pond to gather my seat and backpack, I remember the shot I heard down in the orchard. The waning moments of daylight usher in an even heavier rain. Working my way up the hill, I see headlights at the road. The others have gathered at the trucks, ready to leave.

"Where's John?" I ask them, still huffing and puffing from my walk up the driveway.

"He shot at a doe down in the orchard but thinks he missed," Mike says.

"We looked for blood but didn't find any."

"Is he still looking?"

"I think he's on his way out."

Wanting to walk off some frustration, I dig in my pack for the flashlight and head toward the orchard. When I find John coming up the trail, he's shaking his head, clearly angry.

"Joel, I was right on her . . . she was angling away . . . can't believe she didn't go down."

There were three does. He followed their tracks down into the creek bottom where they'd gone after the shot. "No blood."

"I'll come back tomorrow and look again," he says, staring back toward the brook.

"Do you really think you hit her?"

"She didn't flinch or show any sign of being hit, but the shot seemed *so* good."

"If you think you hit her, let's find her tonight before the sign gets washed away."

"There's not much sign now."

John and I easily follow the tracks where the deer last walked, finding freshly kicked-up leaves and the occasional hoofprint. Descending into the dark, hemlock-strewn creek bottom, the tracks eventually cross the brook and continue up the steep bank on the opposite side. I hike up the bank but can find only two sets of tracks. Walking back up to the orchard, we retrace the tracks again. This time we each get on one side of the trail, painstakingly looking for where one of the deer might have headed in another direction. Still, there's no blood. Nothing. Again the tracks lead us to the brook. Back up we go.

This time, John stays at the orchard, trying to get his bearings and making sure we're on the right set of tracks. Following the sparse sign back to the brook, I walk farther up the opposite side this time. On my way back down, I notice a patch of kicked-up leaves, just off the trail where the deer crossed the brook. Shining my flashlight around the black woods, I find another kicked-up patch, about the size of a pie plate. The little penlight is dimming, threatening to go out. I just about fall over when I find myself looking at two pinpoints of light.

Deer eyes.

As I round an ancient hemlock trunk, relief pours over me. Lying against the tree is the dead doe. Never crossing the brook, it just veered off from the others and died, only a few seconds after John's shot. The only blood is a small patch right next to the deer. I'm excited, relieved, ecstatic, and—most of all—feel I just made up for missing the doe in the field. Putting my hand on the deer's warm back, I savor the moment, listening to John walk around the opening above me.

"John," I say, raising my voice just enough for him to hear me over the noisy brook.

"What?" he asks flatly, unable to hide his frustration.

"You want this deer?"

"*What?*" This time his voice is filled with incredulity. He covers the fifty yards to me in a matter of seconds, stumbling over rocks and cracking branches on his way down. The rain falls steadily around us as I hold our penlights for John to dress out the deer. Looking up from his work, he says, "I owe you for this."

I'm just so thrilled we recovered the deer, I can't think of a thing to say in reply. "You'll get your chance to pay me back—don't worry."

November 20—Payback Time

Sometime during the night, probably early, the temperature dropped and the heavy rain turned to heavier snow. Nestled in a hollow spot against the base of a hemlock tree, I watch helplessly as my backpack is blanketed with snow. This stand of hemlocks, a perfectly square block of trees near the brook, always seems to attract deer during storms. But as the morning wears on, it becomes apparent the deer have found a better spot in which to take refuge today. I haven't seen anything but a gray squirrel, which quickly peeked out at the snow and immediately ducked back into its hole. Perhaps the deer moved down into the hemlocks by the brook, where Steve is. He and Howard are leaving in the afternoon, so I hope he gets one this morning.

I tried radioing John when I heard a shot, but either the topography or the snow kept my signal from getting through. He's in my ground blind, a quarter mile away, and Howard is somewhere on the back line again. I'd like to see him fill his doe tag before he leaves, but I pray he does it on the way out, not when he's back there. My shoulders still ache from the last drag.

Around nine-thirty the snow dissipates, quickly giving way to bright sunshine and a clear blue sky. The wind also picks up,

Howard with his spike buck.

howling across the mountainside. My radio crackles quietly in my ear. Then again. And again. I can't make out anything. Looking around carefully, I slide up out of the hollow, so my headset is clear of the ground.

"John? Steve?" I whisper, "Anybody home?"

John's voice is startlingly loud in my earpiece and I hurry to turn the volume down.

"Steve got a doe."

As I nestle back into the hollow, the woods are flooded with sunlight and the snow on the branches is blinding. Several turkeys appear on the other side of the brook, coming steadily closer. Not doing their normal stop, peck and scratch, they trot along hurriedly. *Howard must be coming.* Maybe some deer will come out, too. Hunkering down in my hollow, I watch and wait. I begin to count the turkeys passing fifty yards away on the opposite side of the brook. Before long, Howard appears, a small red blob in the thick underbrush. The few turkeys still within sight take flight, clumsily departing the hemlock stand.

"I was following fresh turkey tracks the whole way," Howard says, out of breath from his walk. "There had to be at least thirty of them."

"Thirty-six."

"That's *a lot* of turkey meat. Maybe you should have picked off a couple of them," he says, gently ribbing me about not getting a deer yet.

"Maybe."

We spend the remainder of the morning putting on drives. Everyone has filled a tag this rifle season except me, so I'm given the honor of being a "sitter." The first drive is a wicked push through some blue spruces and white pines. The cover is so thick the drivers can't see or hear one another. The deer tend to circle around, in and out of the trees, never exiting to the standers. There are two good places to sit on the drive. One is the Dog Seat. The other is in a huge old beech that snapped off six feet up, leaving a natural platform to stand on. Last year, Greta's brother-in-law sat there and missed a beautiful buck on this drive, so that's where I elect to sit. I'm the only sitter with a headset, listening intently as Howard, John, and Steve make their way through the pines toward Mike and me. There is a lot of confusion as the drivers try to stay on an even keel. That's why they aren't carrying rifles.

A good hard drag is better than no drag at all.

The first two deer appear a hundred yards away, running full tilt. My heart sinks as they not only run toward the vacant Dog Seat but jump *over* the rock I would have been sitting on! Just as Steve appears in the edge of the spruces, five more deer dash out in front of him, racing toward me. But they stop short and turn, also running past the Dog Seat.

Damn.

Walking back to the trucks, we find the tracks of seven other deer that slipped out the side of the drive where no one was watching. The spruces must have been loaded with them. All of the deer escaped down into the bowl, and we discuss doing a quick drive through it. But, checking our watches, we realize we have to get down to the house to get Howard and Steve's deer quartered so they can get on the road.

Among the friends gathered around the little butchering tree in the side yard, the stories fly and the faces are filled with laughter. The knives work quickly, and the coolers fill up just as quickly with this winter's supply of venison. As I work, my mind wanders and I start to get the feeling I'm not going to get a deer this year. Although I killed one with the bow, it's starting to look like the second straight year of rifle hunting with no success. Though there's meat in the freezer, I just don't want to go through the whole winter thinking about my botched shot at the doe. It has to end better than that.

In the afternoon, Doc meets us in the driveway, chiding me when I tell him about missing the doe. He suggests that we go around the pond again to see if anything is feeding in the sunshine. Sneaking up around the pond, we don't see any deer.

John offers to put on a one-man drive through the spruces again, with me seated on the dog stand this time. I agree, knowing that if any deer run past me, it will be a stroke of pure luck. We've already driven this today, and I doubt the deer would have returned yet. Also, there are many other escape routes they could use, if John can get them to move at all. Many times, we've driven these same pines with three or even four guys and had the deer circle back on us. I suggest we use the radios. Since John is less familiar with the drive than I am, I can help him if he gets turned around.

Ten minutes into the drive, I know we're already in trouble.

"OK, Joel. I'm at the barn."

My hopes for shooting a deer sink even further. "OK, John, put your *back* to the barn and walk *away* from it."

This is *not* good.

A few minutes later: "Joel, the sun is at my right shoulder now."

"John, it's at my right shoulder too."

He's walking away from me again! I put my chin in my hand, exasperated, shifting my weight on the cold rock seat. The drive is

So tell me, how'd you get it?

blown. John isn't lost but has probably driven the deer away from me. Straining to see uphill and into the pines, I hear a sudden commotion to my right. Two deer appear. Unbelievably, they're coming from *behind* me, running *into* the pines. I have no time to think. The first deer passes me at fifteen yards, a giant doe. I simultaneously spin to my right and lift the rifle. Seeing movement, the doe makes its final leap into the pines before I can get the hammer back. The deer behind it, however—another doe—skids to a halt behind a beech tree, freezing. It is only ten yards from me, but all I can see is its rump. I hold the cross hairs at the opposite side of the tree trunk for a long time. When the doe finally peeks out, I shoot, dropping it.

John emerges from the same direction the does had come. Whatever he's done—and wherever he's been—he pushed the deer to me. Shaking my hand as he looks down at the doe, he's as happy as I am.

"I told you you'd get to pay me back."

"And all I had to do was get lost!"

"Whatever works," I say, remembering how I stumbled onto his doe down in the dark ravine.

Payback complete.

November 21—Last Day on the Hill

The temptation is to leave early and get on the road. We could be home by dark. But John and I have buck tags to fill, and yesterday's unexpected success helps us decide to stay and hunt a few more hours in the morning. I don't want to sit because I know the whole time I'm sitting, I'll be stewing about the long ride home. I want to do some more proactive hunting, and John agrees. I formulated a plan lying in bed last night, staring at the ceiling with my belly full of fresh venison. I was unable to sleep with John snoring noisily in the basement.

When John calls on the radio to tell me he's in place on my rock pile, I push up into the thick spruces. I'm thankful I left my rifle at the truck as I fight my way through the dense branches. Snow flies in all directions, and several unseen grouse thunder off ahead of me. No wonder the deer like it in here. Here and there,

I cross their runways. Most are trampled deep into the rocky dirt, now lightly covered with the snow that survived yesterday's sun. Finding two fresh beds—apparently those of large deer—I follow the tracks out of them, hoping to get lucky. Breaking into a small clearing in the trees, I suddenly see deer all around me. I notice spike antlers on one as they crash down the hill. I think there are five of them, but they disappear too quickly for me to be sure.

"Buck," I grunt into the mouthpiece of my radio. Sprinting down the hill, I try to head the deer off before they can escape into The Bowl. Needles and branches whack my face as I abandon stealth in favor of speed.

"Where are you? Where's the buck?" John whispers into my ear.

Out of breath, I can't answer him as I fight my way down toward the pond, finally breaking out into the open eighty yards to the east of John. The five sets of deer tracks plow down around the pond, disappearing into The Bowl. Keeping a stand of pines between themselves and the opening, the deer never gave John even a glimpse.

"Where are they?" John's voice crackles insistently.

"They're gone. Down below."

"Damn. Yesterday they would've run right over me!"

"Trust me, I know the feeling."

The Last Push

The woods are beautiful this morning. The valley, still shaded from the rising sun, is ten degrees colder than the world above. The sunlight on the high beech ridges appears occasionally through a break in the hemlock canopy. The wind howls across the ridge, and the whole mountain smells clean, new.

Rising slowly after ten minutes of soaking in the scenery and the smells, I walk across the steep ridge toward John. A few steps in the quiet needles, dotted here and there with snow, and I am once again forced down by the sight of turkeys. Ten of them, running straight up the deer trail I've been backtracking. Putting and gobbling, they are extremely agitated. John must be right behind them. I hide myself behind the nearest big hemlock just as they crest a knoll twenty-five yards from me. There are suddenly turkeys streaming on both sides of me. Two of them spot me and take off flying, their wings nearly hitting me in the face. I've never been so close to them, and my heart is pounding. The remaining birds in the flock sense something is wrong and cut down toward the brook, avoiding me. When they have exited the area, I duck back around to the other side of the tree, facing where John should be coming out. I'm stunned by the sight of a deer hurrying down the trail toward me. Seeing

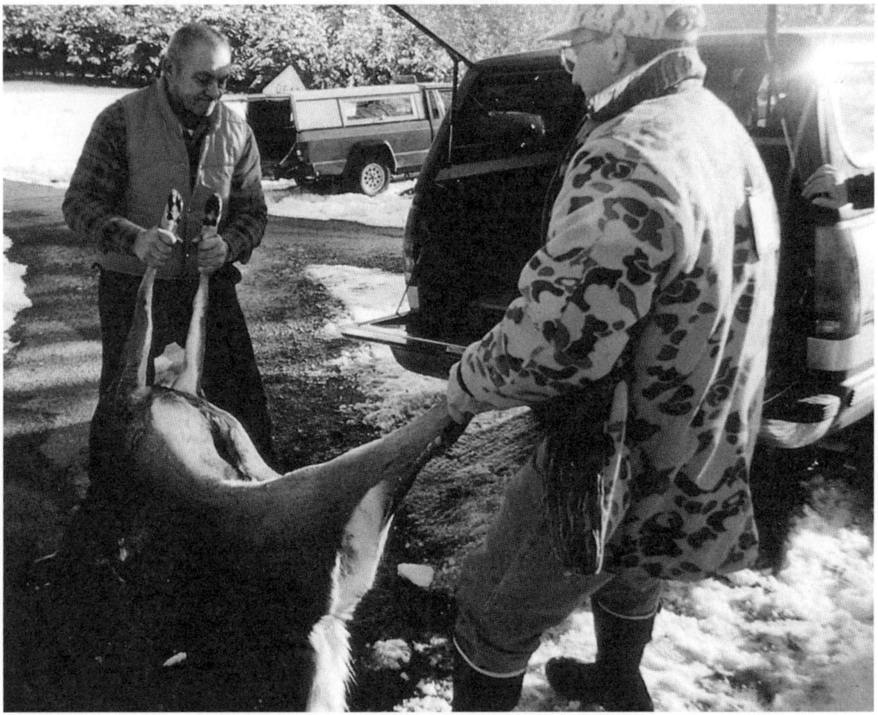

Now the real work begins.

me just as I see it, the deer freezes for an instant, no more than twenty yards away. If I wanted, I could drop it in its tracks, but it's just a little button-buck. Adjusting its course rapidly, it splashes down through the brook, sprinting up the opposite bank into the orchard.

Sitting back against the tree, I wait for John to appear, hoping he'll push more deer out ahead of him. When he finally emerges, I'm surprised when he says he saw the turkeys but not the deer. I don't understand how he could possibly have seen the birds but not seen the button-buck who was in *between* the gobblers and him. Sharing a brief laugh, we agree that it's time to go.

Stopping the car on the way off the hill, we take one last look over at Doc's farm, nestled snugly against the mountain. It will be many long months before we see the sight again. Once back on the main road, it's sad to watch the mountains retreating in the distance. The venison we take home will sustain us through the winter. But the other things I bring back—less tangible things stashed in the deep recesses of my heart, treasures I've been entrusted with, memories, still young and unformed—will nourish me far longer.

THE AFTERSEASON

Winding down, the season bids farewell.
Part of me, the tired part, is glad.
Something else, deeper down, is not. . . .

November 25—Greta's Drive

The last few days have been fruitless. It's been hard to get in the spirit of deer hunting back home after spending the week in the mountains. Any wood lot we drive has probably been driven by another group of hunters already. The past two days have been especially discouraging. Every place we go, we run into other hunters. Many are willing to join up with us, or have us join them, but after spending the week with our tight little group in the Catskills, it just isn't the same.

I've been spoiled.

Today is different, though. Breaking through the brush in the narrow little wood lot next to John's house, I have a good feeling. Not because of the abundant sign or the trampled runways. Not because we chased three deer in here yesterday. Not because the weather is perfect and there's a dusting of fresh snow. Today is different because it's the first time Greta has hunted with me since the first of September—the very start of the season. So much has happened since then, it seems it must have been years ago, not merely months. I guess you don't really know how life has piled up around you until you stop to sort it out.

Two sets of tracks lead into the brush. Crossing the road, I see they came from the bigger wood lot. There's a faint trace of snow in the hoofprints and it only stopped snowing an hour ago. The tracks are fresh—*very* fresh. Rather than walk directly toward

Greta, I follow the sneaking tracks back through the brush. The thin ice under the snow cracks, giving way under my feet, soaking my boots. Making a sharp turn to the south, the tracks start circling. I spot the first bed the same time I spot Brian. Halfway down the thicket he'll join me in driving the rest of the way to Greta. Bending over the bigger of the two deer beds, I notice tracks leading out of it. Taking a few more steps to see where the deer broke through the ice, I see the snow spattered with muddy water droplets. It dawns on me that the deer were probably lying right here when Brian walked up to the edge of the thicket, and they slipped away right under his nose. From his angle, he couldn't have seen them through the brush. Motioning to him, I try to relay to him that I'm going to the far edge of the thicket to cut the deer off. I signal for him to work straight toward Greta. With any luck, the deer are still trapped between the three of us.

When I break out of the brush into the mowed grass of John's neighbor's field, Greta is running down the edge toward me, gesturing wildly and pointing across the field.

Uh-oh.

Breathlessly, she says a lone doe shot out right ahead of me, too far for a shot. It occurs to me that there is still another deer in the brush, but after looking for the tracks, we find that it cut back between Brian and me, crossing the road into the bigger wood lot again. *Very* sneaky, indeed. I can't help wondering if it's a buck.

Following the bounding tracks of Greta's doe across the field, we enter a stand of pines on the other side. There's a huge drainage ditch there, and I'm willing to bet that since we didn't chase the doe right away, it didn't try to cross. If it turned up the ditch and is walking up to the natural crossing several hundred yards up, there's a chance we can intercept it there. Greta and Brian hurry to the end of the field. When they disappear inside the pines, I step into the shady woods. Hoping they are ready, I don't wait. If we're going to pin this deer down, it's going to have to be quick. After only a few steps, I cross the doe's tracks. Once it got inside the woods, it stopped bounding and started walking. That's a good sign. Unfortunately, the tracks continue toward the deep ditch. Following the doe's footsteps, I try to follow its thoughts as well. The tracks go directly up to the edge of the steep bank of the ditch and stop. I envision the deer standing there, gauging the jump across the water. The bank is six feet above the water and is nearly vertical. A missed jump, and it would land head over hooves. It'd end up like Phil did.

The doe, at least, had enough sense not to jump.

The tracks continue down along the bank, as it looked for a more opportune place to cross. I see where its hooves dug into the bank as it launched itself across the ditch. It almost made it, but there's a broken patch of ice on the opposite side where muddy water is splashed up the bank. The doe dug hard in as it scrambled up the steep bank, and dirt is spread all over the broken ice. I admire the animal's tenacity. A younger, more foolish deer might have waited inside the pines, but this one wasted no time. It escaped into a narrow corridor of brush that runs down along a creek, toward the goose field. Greta and Brian join me, shaking their heads in amazement at the sight of the doe's leap across the deep ditch.

Brian offers to drive the creek bottom to us, and we agree to use the radios this time. Driving quickly to the woods near the goose field, Greta and I take up positions at the end of the brushy creek. We talk quietly on the radio as Brian makes the long hike up through the brush. We don't hear from him for twenty minutes. I'm not surprised, since the creek is a brushy nightmare.

When Brian's voice finally crackles through on the radio, a half-hour has passed. He tells us that after the doe crossed the brook, she never stopped running. She bounded the whole way down the creek bottom. Smart deer. Brian finally lost her tracks as they mixed in with other deer sign along the creek bank. As we wait for him to emerge, there's one hopeful moment when we hear branches breaking in the thick brush. *Deer?*

What comes out is a tired, brush-beaten Brian.

There will be other little drives and hunts over the next week or so, but as I unload the shotgun and lay it in the back of the truck, the excitement of the season is over for me. I'll go on a few duck hunts with John, Jay, and Tom in the coming weeks, but the migration won't be as it is predicted to be. We'll shoot a few ducks and share stories. But mostly the memories of those hunts will be about standing in the cold river in the predawn hours, with pinpoints of light up the river showing us the lanterns of others as foolish as we. Sitting and shivering on the bank of the river, day in and day out for a week, I'll be thinking about September, about the goose field. My mind will reel back to past winters, when the ducks all seemed to fly into our decoys. The days when our wingshooting was better and the ducks crumpled at the sound of the guns. But maybe those memories have been damaged in storage. Maybe those days weren't so good.

I choose to believe they *were*.

I'll take Maggie and Ted out a few times for rabbits. Though we'll manage to shoot a few, the excitement of bird season is forgotten. Every now and then, the dogs will get on pheasant scent and their excitement will be back, but even Maggie and Ted know this kind of hunting is just a pale reminder, a cheap imitation of October. The golden fields of our dreams will be hidden under a perpetual blanket of white, and no matter how hard we try to make their colors shine through the snow, we know only time can do that.

And time takes time.

Standing by the edge of the goose field, Greta, Brian, and I talk about the doe, reminiscing about our other adventures here over the past few years. The talk is light, the conversation affectionate and taunting in a way only friends know. This is the kind of moment that will whisper in my memory in the coming year, when the season seems a lifetime away. As Greta takes my hand and the three of us hike into the field, I know we've been blessed. Allowed to take part in the eternal rituals of life and death, we have again been shown the elemental truths found in both.

There is wisdom in the honking of the geese, knowledge in the singing of the coyotes. What these wild ones know is nothing that can be passed along on paper, though. They are lessons that must be studied with your back to a cold tree or moss-covered rock, or with a good dog curled up against your leg for warmth. They are lessons that are meant not to be learned, but to be lived.

March 1

As I walk unenthusiastically into work after a long break, Brian meets me at the office door.

"Won't be long now," he says.

"What won't be?" I ask, envisioning some devastating company layoff.

He points over his shoulder to the calendar on the wall. "Only eight more months to bird season. It's coming fast."

I shake my head sadly, laughing as I look down at my work boots. When I look up, though, Brian's not laughing.

He's dead serious.

April 3

The venison is delicious. Next to me at the table, Jessica, my six-year-old daughter, is wolfing it down in dangerously large bites.

"Think she likes it?" Greta asks me from across the table.

"I think so."

"This is really tender. Which deer is it?" I ask, thinking it must have come from the small doe I shot during rifle season.

Greta walks out into the kitchen and holds up the wrapper.

October 15, buck, it says in black marker on the white freezer paper.

Drifting back to the opening day of bow season, I remember the long crawl across Doc's side yard. I remember the surprised look on the buck's face as I reared up from behind the stone wall and let the arrow fly. I remember the overwhelming feeling of sadness as I watched it run away, its death—by my hand—imminent.

For a moment, that sadness returns, and I hang my head and silently give thanks, promising myself I'll remember to do so more often.

June 14

Sifting through my fly-tying supplies, I set aside all kinds of odd stuff in an effort to get at what I'm looking for. There are squirrel tails in every size and shape. There are dry-fly hackle necks by the handful, some that cost a buck or two, and some that cost—let's just say they were spirited into the house under cover of darkness. There are furs and feathers and threads and tinsels and hooks and on and on and on. But I still can't find what I've been looking for.

I could have sworn I put them there, but the bottom of the last of my half-dozen boxes doesn't produce them. I remember now. They're in the workshop. Screwing in the light bulb, I look into the floor joists above the hot-water heater. Right next to the eight-point set of antlers I picked up in Maine is a handful of pheasant tail feathers I put there back in October. They're what I need to tie my trout flies.

Taking down the bunch of feathers, I brush cobwebs off them, holding them up to my nose. The smell is rich and wild. Even after all these months, the rooster is still there. I'm suddenly back in the field with Brian, chasing the dogs all over creation, finally nailing this bird down in the hedgerow. We flushed the bird three times, if I recall right, finally catching him in a last-minute flush. *Oh, that was fun.* The memory floods back, momentarily washing away the thoughts and worries that have filled my mind lately. I close my eyes and see every detail of that day.

The season is right there, just under the surface. *Always.*

Turning to take the feathers back to my tying table, I nearly trip over Maggie. Wagging her stubby tail, she looks up at me. As I hold out one of the big tail feathers, she puts her front paws on my thigh, stretching to sniff at the remains of her rooster. Taking a long smell of the feathers, she looks off to one side, staring into space, thinking. She's back in October, too.

"Won't be long now, Maggie," I say, ruffling the curly hair between her ears. "It's just around the corner."